Endorsements

What is most often missing in discipleship and Bible study materials is attention to the overarching story of the Bible (what literary scholars call the metanarrative). *The Big Story* specifically addresses this omission by focusing on the big picture of Scripture while not neglecting the smaller portraits. This curriculum is designed in such a way that is both advantageous to teachers and accessible to students from any background and any educational level. Moreover, the material presented is thoroughly biblical and theologically sound. *The Big Story* provides an extremely useful tool to help the laborers of Christ disciple the nations.

Jim Fitzgerald, Master of Arts in Theological Studies, Reformed Theological Seminary
Director of Missions, Middle East and North Africa, Equipping Pastors International

The Big Story is an invaluable resource. Few Bible study guides present so broad and sweeping a picture of salvation history. The book is oriented to seekers and believers at any stage; and although it was designed to be used in small groups, I think it would even be useful in one-on-one meetings. I found the questions in each chapter to be engaging and well-designed for stimulating conversation. The leaders' guide was also very well done and gives the leader a great resource to lead a discussion. Overall, I'm very impressed with *The Big Story*—Its solid biblical foundation and usefulness for both evangelism and discipleship.

Jim Cunningham, Master of Divinity
Regional Director, North Asia, Young Life

THE BIG STORY

THE GREATER SACRIFICE

CHRISTOPHER STONE

WESTBOW
PRESS®
A DIVISION OF THOMAS NELSON
& ZONDERVAN

Copyright © 2023 Christopher Stone.

All rights reserved. No part of this book may be used or reproduced by any means, graphic, electronic, or mechanical, including photocopying, recording, taping or by any information storage retrieval system without the written permission of the author except in the case of brief quotations embodied in critical articles and reviews.

This book is a work of non-fiction. Unless otherwise noted, the author and the publisher make no explicit guarantees as to the accuracy of the information contained in this book and in some cases, names of people and places have been altered to protect their privacy.

WestBow Press books may be ordered through booksellers or by contacting:

WestBow Press
A Division of Thomas Nelson & Zondervan
1663 Liberty Drive
Bloomington, IN 47403
www.westbowpress.com
844-714-3454

Because of the dynamic nature of the Internet, any web addresses or links contained in this book may have changed since publication and may no longer be valid. The views expressed in this work are solely those of the author and do not necessarily reflect the views of the publisher, and the publisher hereby disclaims any responsibility for them.

Scripture quotations marked ESV are from the ESV Bible® (The Holy Bible, English Standard Version®), copyright © 2001 by Crossway Bibles, a publishing ministry of Good News Publishers. Used by permission. All rights reserved.

Unless cited otherwise, all Scripture quotations are taken from the NIV, New International Version®, NIV®. Copyright © 1973, 1978, 1984 by Biblica, Inc.™ Used by permission of Zondervan. All rights reserved worldwide.

Scripture quotations marked NKJV are taken from the New King James Version. Copyright © 1982 by Thomas Nelson, Inc. Used by permission. All rights reserved.

ISBN: 978-1-6642-9620-6 (sc)
ISBN: 978-1-6642-9622-0 (hc)
ISBN: 978-1-6642-9621-3 (e)

Library of Congress Control Number: 2023906203

Print information available on the last page.

WestBow Press rev. date: 07/27/2023

To my covenant bride in Christ Jesus and gospel partner
in life and death for the glory of God's name
"I am my beloved's and my beloved is mine."
(Song of Solomon 6:3)

CONTENTS

Preface ix
Acknowledgements xi
Introduction xiii

Lesson 1   The Image of God 1
Lesson 2   Fall of the Kingdom 10
Lesson 3   Kingdom Exile 21
Lesson 4   Covenant Faith 34
Lesson 5   Burnt Offering 45
Lesson 6   Kingdom Law Explained 56
Lesson 7   Promise of the Son-King 67
Lesson 8   Prophecy of the Servant-King 77
Lesson 9   Revelation of the King 86
Lesson 10   Kingdom Law Fulfilled 97
Lesson 11   Sacrifice of the King 106
Lesson 12   Exaltation of the King 117

Appendix I: Gospel Invitation 127
Glossary 131
Bibliography 137

PREFACE

It was the winter of 2015. We were huddled around the fire, seeking warmth and light, amid the chilled darkness of the sub-Saharan night. We were gospel journeymen, being trained in storytelling and sent out into surrounding villages with the precious light of truth. From this seminal experience, a burning passion to bring the gospel narrative of scripture to light began to glow within me.

Several months later, I traveled again to the Far East. Here, I gained experience in leading Bible studies in the ESL (English as a Second Language) community. In 2018, the Father sparked within me the idea of merging narrative storytelling of the gospel with English literacy. My teammate and I crafted lessons and began a Bible study with ESL learners. What began as an informal Bible study grew into a larger project that garnered the attention of one of my organization's leaders.

When I transitioned to the Middle East in 2019, I was tasked to lead a small team to fully develop a Bible study curriculum that traced the big story of Christ from Genesis to Revelation and that provided English learning aids and strategies for the ESL community in which we lived and taught. From this larger work, we now present a condensed format from Genesis to the Gospels.

The aim of this book is twofold. First, we desire to grow and train disciples of Christ to understand the main thrust of the narrative of scripture and to know God more intimately through the study of Christ in both the Old and New Testaments. Second, we desire to provide the ESL community with a ready-made English-learning curriculum that showcases Christ in the fullness of His glory through His person and work from the promises of the Old Testament. While some elements of the curriculum focus on ESL learners, this curriculum is not limited to ESL learners. It is for all who would take up His word and read.

ACKNOWLEDGEMENTS

Due to the sensitive areas in which we work, I will only describe but not name the many hands that have played a part in this project.

I am deeply indebted to my teammate who believed in me and worked with me to develop the first draft.

I am intensely thankful for my organization's leaders and the Big Story team for their kingdom investment in this project. Their suggested improvements, English curriculum creation, and editing expertise have elevated this curriculum from its humble beginnings.

I am beholden to my wife, even before marriage, who worked tirelessly to edit the ever-changing manuscripts without complaint.

I also am profoundly grateful for my organization's support for this project and the many donors that made it possible.

INTRODUCTION

What is the Big Story and why is it so big?

Because this is the most important story we have ever heard, we think it is important for people to hear it. It is a story God has told us in many ways about who He is, who we are, and why it matters that we know Him. As we read scripture, we cannot help but see that God loves a good story! Scripture is filled with many kinds of stories that once entertained the listening ear in oral-based cultures. These stories, having been faithfully recorded, now captivate hearts and minds. This study is designed not to look at all the details but to look at the big story, a collection of stories encased in God's larger narrative.

What resources will I find about the Big Story here?

We have created a collection of lessons that help us listen to a small part of the Big Story. Each lesson includes a review discussion and usually a review activity; a short vocabulary list to highlight key definitions; an introduction with a lesson purpose and lesson context; the lesson with passages and a discussion in two or three parts; and a wrap-up with the purpose statement for the lesson, a general reflection question, and a key lesson question. These lessons can be discussed in multiple contexts, whether small group, one-on-one, or individual. The definitions in the lessons are intentionally limited to the context of the word in the passage. While the words often will have different meanings in other contexts, this study does not provide general definitions that would fit all usages but specific definitions to the context in which it is used.

Each lesson also comes with a Leader Guide and Lesson Materials. The Leader Guide provides an objective statement and a response statement. In addition, it includes answers to the discussion questions and breakout pivots and details information to help a leader facilitate a discussion and lead the learners to understand the meaning of the passage. The questions with an asterisk (*) in the Leader Guide indicate core questions that highlight the most important ideas in the lesson, which hold the story together and drive the story toward its intended conclusion. Make sure you focus on these questions during the lesson.

Lesson Materials is linked to the Leader Guide and includes three sections: Review Activity; Breakout Pivot; and Additional Resources. The Review Activity provides learners with additional practice that prompts them to interact visually with key concepts in a smaller group setting. The Breakout Pivot also changes the grouping from one group to smaller groups of two or three to discuss a specific chart that incrementally builds different themes from lesson to lesson. Additional Resources contains all the additional resources needed for the lesson, including charts and answer keys. You can access Lesson Materials by scanning the QR code in the Leader Guide.

The Meditation helps learners continue to think about and work with the knowledge they learned in the lesson. You will discover the following elements: key memory verse(s), the space to respond to the key lesson question, concept questions, and reflection questions. The Meditation is helpful for both first and second language English speakers. You can access the Meditation for the lesson by scanning the QR code at the end of the lesson.

The Introduction prepares learners for the next lesson. You will have access to the Lesson Vocabulary, which includes a key vocabulary list and a supplemental vocabulary list. You will be prompted to read the passage and engage in activities that will introduce you to the content of the lesson, prepare you for an important thematic element in the lesson, and give you practice with review vocabulary and concepts. This will be particularly useful for learners who may struggle with some of the English vocabulary needed to aid in comprehension. You can access the Introduction for the next lesson by scanning the QR code at the end of the lesson.

In addition to the resources for each lesson, we have also provided resources to help you become more familiar with the curriculum. For a scope and sequence of the curriculum, scan this QR code:

For a more detailed explanation of the theology and methodology of the Big Story as well as specific instructions on how to lead a study, listen to the "Training Materials" episodes of *The Big Story Study Podcast*. For an audio clip of each lesson, listen to episodes 1–12. You can access *The Big Story Study Podcast* by scanning this QR code:

Finally, we would love to hear about your experience using this curriculum. If you have any questions or would like to send feedback on your experience, please contact us through the following email address: info@bigstorystudy.com.

LESSON 1
The Image of God

Study Introduction

1. Share a brief self-introduction including your name, where you are from, and something about your family, job, school, etc.

2. What is your experience learning about the Bible? Have you studied it before, and if so what / how long? What have you learned about it?

3. Why do you want to study now, and what are you hoping to learn or get from this time together?

4. Do you have any questions you hope are answered before the end of all the lessons?

Lesson Introduction

Purpose: To understand who God is, who people are, and how people are related to God, each other, and creation

Genesis Context: Genesis is the first book found in the Bible. It is one of five books written by Moses about the creation and early history of the world.

Psalms Context: Psalms was written in the style of poetry and songs so that the people of God would see God's beauty, remember truth about God, and worship God as the true King in His beauty and majesty.

Vocabulary

- God: The only true God, Creator, and Judge who is separate from everything else and better than everything else

- Image: Something or someone that represents the honor, authority, or reputation of someone else

- Lord: The personal name of God that shows Him as having a close relationship with man

- Lord/Sovereign: The name of God that shows Him as the King with complete authority over all that He created

- Represent: To act or speak officially for someone or something

- Shame: Loss of respect or honor; a feeling of embarrassment because you have done something wrong

- Son of man: The ruler who represents mankind to God and establishes the rule of God over the earth

Part I: Image of God in Man (Genesis 1:1, 26–31)

In the beginning God created the heavens and the earth…and the Spirit of God was hovering over the waters…²⁶ Then God said, "Let us make mankind in our image, in our likeness…²⁷ so God created mankind in his own image, in the image of God he created them; male and female he created them. ²⁸ God blessed them and said to them, "Be fruitful and increase in number; fill the earth and subdue it. Rule over the fish in the sea and the birds in the sky and over every living creature that moves on the ground. ²⁹ Then God said, "I give you every seed-bearing plant on the face of the whole earth and every tree that has fruit with seed in it. They will be yours for food. ³⁰ And to all the beasts of the earth and all the birds of the air and all the creatures that move on the ground—everything that has the breath of life in it—I give every green plant for food." And it was so. ³¹ God saw all that he had made, and it was very good.

Psalm 8

O Lord, our Lord, how majestic is your name in all the earth! You have set your glory above the heavens…³ When I look at your heavens, the work of your fingers, the moon and the stars, which you have set in place, ⁴ what is man that you are mindful of him, and the son of man that you care for him? ⁵ Yet you have made him a little lower than the heavenly beings and crowned him with glory and honor. ⁶ You have given him dominion over the works of your hands; you have put all things under his feet, ⁷ all sheep and oxen, and also the beasts of the field, ⁸ the birds of the heavens, and the fish of the sea, whatever passes along the paths of the seas. ⁹ O Lord, our Lord, how majestic is your name in all the earth!

Discussion

1. What did God do?
2. What did God tell mankind to do?
3. What was the relationship like between God and mankind?
4. What similar information is given in the second passage? Is there any additional information we can see?

5. Who is God? What is God's relationship to mankind?
6. Who is mankind? What does God give to mankind?
   - What is mankind's relationship to God?
   - What is mankind's relationship to creation?

Part II: Responsibilities of Man (Genesis 2:7–9, 15–17)

Then the Lord God formed a man from the dust of the ground and breathed into his nostrils the breath of life, and the man became a living being. ⁸ Now the Lord God had planted a garden in the east, in Eden; and there he put the man he had formed. ⁹ The Lord God made all kinds of trees grow out of the ground—trees that were pleasing to the eye and good for food. In the middle of the garden were the tree of life and the tree of the knowledge of good and evil…¹⁵ The Lord God took the man and put him in the Garden of Eden to work it and take care of it. ¹⁶ And the Lord God commanded the man, "You are free to eat from any tree in the garden; ¹⁷ but you must not eat from the tree of the knowledge of good and evil, for when you eat from it you will certainly die."

Discussion

1. What was in the middle of the garden?
2. What did God want man to do in the garden?
   - What does working the garden mean?
   - What does taking care of the garden mean?
     - Subdue/rule/guard
   - **Digging Deeper:** In His kindness and provision, God created a place for man to learn more about Him and how to care for and subdue the earth. Eventually, mankind would *fill* the whole earth, but He provided a garden for them to begin. God intended for mankind to make the rest of the world just like Eden, a place of beauty, peace, and harmony where God is worshipped and obeyed.
3. What one law did God give to the man? What would happen if man disobeyed God's law?

Part III: Relational Nature of Mankind (Genesis 2:18–25)

The Lord God said, "It is not good for the man to be alone. I will make a helper suitable for him." ¹⁹Now the Lord God had formed out of the ground all the wild animals and all the birds in the sky. He brought them to the man to see what he would name them; and whatever the man called each living creature, that was its name. [20] So the man gave names to all the livestock, the birds in the sky and all the wild animals. But for Adam no suitable helper was found.[21] So the LORD God caused the man to fall into a deep sleep; and while he was sleeping, he took one of the man's ribs and then closed up the place with flesh. [22] Then the LORD God made a woman from the rib he had taken out of the man, and he brought her to the man. [23] The man said,

"This is now bone of my bone and flesh of my flesh; she shall be called 'woman,' for she was taken out of man."

[24] That is why a man leaves his father and mother and is united to his wife, and they become one flesh. [25] Adam and his wife were both naked, and they felt no shame.

Discussion

> "So God created mankind in his own image, in the image of God he created them; male and female he created them." (Genesis 1:27)

1. Why did God create women?
2. What relationship did God plan for man and woman? Why?
3. What were some ways God cared for the man and the woman?
4. What were the man and the woman *not* meant to experience?
    - What does shame feel like?
5. What did the man and the woman experience in the garden?
6. How was the Garden of Eden the kingdom of God?

Breakout Pivot: Kingdom Chart

Key Lesson Question: How does being made in the image of God influence how you understand God, yourself, and your purpose in life?

Reminder: Scan this QR code to do the Meditation for this lesson and the Introduction for the next lesson:

Leader Guide

Objective: To describe mankind's relationship to God and aspects of the character of God through God's names and His creation of mankind in His image, examine the differing relationships within the Garden of Eden, and analyze the responsibilities of man and woman to God and to each other

Response: Because I am made in the image of God, I represent God as ruler over His creation and am blessed by God with worth and honor.

Lesson Materials QR Code:

Study Introduction (5–10 minutes): Refer to the lesson.

Lesson Introduction (5 minutes): Refer to Lesson Materials.

Lesson 1 (40–45 minutes)

Part I: Image of God in Man (Genesis 1:1, 26–31; Psalm 8)

1. What did God do? (v. 1) *
   *Note: The Holy Spirit hovering over the waters is a reference to the Holy Spirit participating in the action of creating. Avoid getting into a discussion of the Trinity. Let them know that the Holy Spirit is God and was creating.
   - God created the world and blessed mankind (men and women).

2. What did God tell mankind to do? (v. 28) *
   - Be fruitful, fill the earth, subdue it, and rule over it.

3. What was the relationship like between God and mankind? *
   - The relationship between God and mankind was good. God called His creation of mankind *very good*.
   - God gave them all they needed and blessed them abundantly. They had all the food they needed. They were given purpose and authority. There was peace and goodness.

1. What similar information is given in this second passage? Is there any additional information we can see?
   - Similar: God is Creator; God gave authority to man over creation.
   - Additional: God is described as majestic and is full of glory. God created man with glory and honor.

2. Who is God? What is God's relationship to mankind? *
   *Note: Refer to the **Names of God Chart** from Lesson Materials.
   - **God:** The only true God, Creator, and Judge who is separate from everything else and better than everything else
   - God is the Lord our Lord.
     - ❖ Lord: The name of God that expresses a close relationship. In verse 4, we see that the Lord cares for mankind in a personal way. Also, in Genesis 1, we see that the Lord made mankind in His image. Because mankind was created in the image of God, mankind had a personal relationship with God as Lord.
     - ❖ **Lord:** The name of God that expresses ruling authority over us. We see God's lordship in His authority to create mankind in the way that He decides is good. We see God's authority when God gives directions to mankind and gives mankind the power to rule the earth.
     - ❖ **Summary:** When we combine these two names of God, we discover that God made us to live in close relationship with Him under His rule as King.

3. Who is mankind? What does God give to mankind? (v. 6) *
   *Note: Refer to the **Image of God Chart** from Lesson Materials.
   - Mankind is a creature who is made in God's image (Genesis 1:26–27) who has been given authority to rule, glory, and honor (Psalm 8:5–6).
   - What is mankind's relationship to God?
     - ❖ Mankind was created to bring glory to God. Bringing glory means to give God the respect that He deserves in our behavior and obedience to Him and to worship Him for His greatness. We should honor Him in our actions, thoughts, and behavior.
   - What is mankind's relationship to creation?
     - ❖ According to Psalm 8, God is the highest authority (Lord) but allows mankind to have authority over creation under His rule. God has crowned mankind as ruler over His creation to care for, protect, and govern.

Part II: Responsibilities of Man (Genesis 2:7–9, 15–17)

1. What was in the middle of the garden? (v. 9) *
   - Two trees that were pleasing and good for food: the tree of the knowledge of good and evil and the tree of life

2. What did God want man to do in the garden? (v. 15) *
   - God intended for man to work and take care of the garden.
   - What does working the garden mean?
     - ❖ Man should be fruitful and produce good things.
   - What does taking care of the garden mean? Consider what God told man to do in the first passage:
     *Note: Refer to the **Image of God Chart** from Lesson Materials.
     - ❖ **Subdue** meant they should control the earth with power over creation.
     - ❖ **Rule** meant they have authority over creation to make decisions for creation and rule under God as King, carrying out His commands on the earth.
     - ❖ **Take care/guard** meant he should watch over the Garden of Eden to preserve it as a place of peace and harmony and to take care of the garden by preserving its beauty.
   - **Digging Deeper:** Refer to the lesson.

3. What one law did God give to the man? What would happen if man disobeyed God's law? (v. 17) *
   - Do not eat of the tree of the knowledge of good and evil.
   - Mankind would die.

Part III: Relational Nature of Mankind (Genesis 2:18–25)
*Note: Read Genesis 1:27 in the lesson.

1. Why did God create women? (v. 18)
   - God values relationships, and it is important for man not to be alone. He wanted mankind to experience relationships and help one another. We learned that God created mankind in His image. Both men and women are needed to fully demonstrate the image of God to the earth. God created mankind as male and female to display Himself through these two distinct genders in their unique form (biology) and function.

2. What relationship did God plan for man and woman? Why?
   - God provided a marriage relationship for the man and the woman. In marriage, one man and one woman are united to become one

flesh. God took something from Adam that is now missing and only to be found in woman. God created woman to help man in the work of subduing the earth and caring for the garden and to provide companionship for man and woman in unity, harmony, and joy.

3. What were some ways God cared for the man and the woman? *
   - God put them in a beautiful, fruitful garden; God gave them all kinds of different food; God provided them with the gift of marriage to experience companionship, etc.

4. What were the man and the woman *not* meant to experience? (v. 25) *
   - Shame, loneliness, evil, hunger, death, being covered/fear
   - What does shame feel like?
     - ❖ Feels like: embarrassment, discomfort, not feeling good enough, feeling lesser than

5. What did the man and the woman experience in the garden? *
   - They were free to be who God created them to be without fear of embarrassment. They knew that they were loved. They experienced harmony and peace with God, themselves, and creation. They knew the right thing without hesitation. There was no worry, pain, sickness, or death.

6. How was the Garden of Eden the kingdom of God? *
   - God created mankind in His image to be rulers and blessed them with a close relationship with God, each other, and creation. He commanded mankind to subdue the earth and fill the earth so that the earth submits to God's rule.
   - God crowned Adam as the first son of man. He gave Adam the law of the kingdom. God set up Adam as the caretaker and guardian of Eden.
   - God established peace, creativity, family, work, etc. so that mankind did *not* experience shame, fear, conflict, pain, or death.
   - Provide learners the summary definition for the kingdom of God in the Bible: God's rule through God's people over God's place (adapted from Treat 2019).

THE BIG STORY

Breakout Pivot: Kingdom Chart (5 minutes)

- **Fill in the blank directions:** Separate learners into groups of two or three. Have the students ask each other the questions in the chart to fill in the blanks. The answers are in the word bank on the right side of the chart.
  *Note: First, show them an example; then have them do it.
  - ❖ Learner 1: Where was the place of the kingdom of God?
  - ❖ Learner 2: The place of the kingdom of God was the *Garden of Eden*.
- **Further Explanation:** According to Psalm 8, the son of man is the title for the one who represents mankind to God and establishes the rule of God over the earth. The first man, Adam, is presented as the first son of man who has a special place of authority and rule over all creation. He represented mankind to God and ruled over the kingdom of God. God gave Adam the responsibility to take care of and to guard the kingdom. God gave Adam the law of the kingdom. If Adam obeyed, mankind would be granted access to the tree of life to live forever. If Adam disobeyed, mankind would fall under the curse of death. God created woman from Adam, and Adam named woman. Adam named all the animals. Naming a person or a thing is a function of authority. Adam had authority over all that God created because he represented mankind to God as God's ruler over the earth.
  *Note (leader only): The son of man theme is important to the study because it will lead us to Jesus, who is the ideal Son of Man.

Wrap-up (10–15 minutes)

- Ask learners: What is the purpose of the lesson?
  - ➢ To understand who God is, who people are, and how people are related to God, each other, and creation
- Ask learners: What is one new thing that you learned today?
- State to learners: Think about this **Key Lesson Question:**
  - ➢ How does being made in the image of God influence how you understand God, yourself, and your purpose in life?

LESSON 2
Fall of the Kingdom

Review

1. What are the different names or titles of God that you have seen in the passages from Lesson 1?

2. What is God's relationship to mankind and what is man's relationship to God? What was the relationship like between God and mankind?

3. How does being made in the image of God influence how you understand God, yourself, and your purpose in life?

4. What were the two trees called in the middle of the garden? What command did God give to the man about one of the trees? What would happen if man disobeyed God's command?

5. How was the Garden of Eden the kingdom of God?
   - Definition of the kingdom of God:
   - What did they *not* experience in the garden?

Introduction

Purpose: To understand the consequences of disobeying God's command and how we can have hope in a world of sin and death

Vocabulary

- Corrupt: To damage or destroy something so that it no longer looks like it once did and no longer can do what it was made to do

- Curse: The act of God speaking judgment on sinners because the covenant has been broken

- Death: The state of being removed from God's blessing and placed under His curse

- Enmity: A feeling of strong hate

- Guilt: Responsibility for having done something wrong and especially something against the law (Merriam-Webster 2022)

- Offspring: A person's child

- Sin: To break God's law
- Symbol: A physical sign (event/word/action) that points to something (idea or spiritual truth) greater or someone greater

Part I: Disobeying the Law of God (Genesis 3:1–7)

Now the serpent was more crafty than any of the wild animals the Lord God had made. He said to the woman, "Did God really say, 'You must not eat from any tree in the garden'?" ² The woman said to the serpent, "We may eat fruit from the trees in the garden, ³ but God did say, 'You must not eat fruit from the tree that is in the middle of the garden, and you must not touch it, or you will die.'" ⁴ "You will not certainly die," the serpent said to the woman. ⁵ "For God knows that when you eat from it your eyes will be opened, and you will be like God, knowing good and evil." ⁶ When the woman saw that the fruit of the tree was good for food and pleasing to the eye, and also desirable for gaining wisdom, she took some and ate it. She also gave some to her husband, who was with her, and he ate it. ⁷ Then the eyes of both of them were opened, and they realized they were naked; so they sewed fig leaves together and made coverings for themselves.

Discussion

1. What question did the serpent ask? What do you think was the intention behind this question?
2. What did the snake tell the woman to convince her it was OK to disobey what God commanded?
3. What did the woman think of the fruit from the tree of the knowledge of good and evil?
   - What are some things that feel good but are bad for us?

Part II: Consequences of Guilt (Genesis 3:8–19)

Then the man and his wife heard the sound of the Lord God as he was walking in the garden in the cool of the day, and they hid from the Lord God among the trees of the garden. ⁹ But the Lord God called to the man, "Where are you?" ¹⁰ He answered, "I heard you in the garden, and I was afraid because I was naked; so I hid." ¹¹ And he said, "Who told you that you were naked? Have you eaten from the tree that I commanded you not to eat from?" ¹² The man said, "The woman you put here with me—she gave me some fruit from the tree, and I ate it." ¹³ Then the Lord God said to the woman, "What is this you have done?" The woman said, "The serpent deceived me, and I ate."

¹⁴ So the Lord God said to the serpent, "Because you have done this, "Cursed are you above all livestock and all wild animals! You will crawl on your belly and you will eat dust all the days of your life.

¹⁵ And I will put enmity between you and the woman, and between your offspring and hers; he will crush your head, and you will strike his heel."

¹⁶To the woman he said, "I will make your pains in childbearing very severe; with painful labor you will give birth to children. Your desire will be for your husband, and he will rule over you."

¹⁷ To Adam he said, "Because you listened to your wife and ate fruit from the tree about which I commanded you, 'You must not eat from it,' "Cursed is the ground because of you; through painful toil you will eat food from it all the days of your life. ¹⁸ It will produce thorns and thistles for you, and you will eat the plants of the field. ¹⁹ By the sweat of your brow you will eat your food until you return to the ground, since from it you were taken; for dust you are and to dust you will return."

Discussion

1. What did the man and his wife hear? What does that say about the relationship God had and wanted to have with mankind?
2. What did Adam and Eve do after they ate the fruit?
3. What did they experience for the first time?
    - _____:
    - _____:
    - _____:
4. How do we experience some of the same things as Adam and Eve?
5. What punishments did God give Adam and Eve?
6. What does returning to the ground in verse 19 mean?
    - What did God say would happen if they disobeyed the law?
    - What did the serpent say would happen?
    - What actually happened?

Part III: Provision for Mankind (Genesis 3:20–24)

Adam named his wife Eve, because she would become the mother of all the living. ²¹ The Lord God made garments of skin for Adam and his wife and clothed them. ²² And the Lord God said, "The man has now become like one of us, knowing good and evil. He must not be allowed to reach out his hand and take also from the tree of life and eat, and live forever." ²³ So the Lord God banished him from the Garden of Eden to work the ground from which he had been taken. ²⁴ After he drove the man out, he placed on the east side of the Garden of Eden cherubim and a flaming sword flashing back and forth to guard the way to the tree of life.

Discussion

1. Read verses 23–24. How did the relationship between God and Adam and Eve change?
   - What came into the world for the first time?
   - How do we know Adam and Eve were guilty from the passage?
   - **Digging Deeper:** How does Adam's guilt affect us today?
2. Read verse 21. What did God provide for Adam and Eve? Does He still care for them?
   - What were the clothes made of? What do you think this means?
3. Read verse 15. What is the relationship between the woman's Offspring and the serpent?
   - What do they do to each other?
   - What hope does God give to mankind?

Overarching Themes

Verse	Overarching Theme	Lesson # Emphasis
Genesis 3:15	The Promise of the Offspring that defeats sin and death	#4, 6, 7, 9, 10, 12
Genesis 3:21	The Sacrifice that covers shame and removes guilt	#4, 5, 8, 11

Key Lesson Question: In what ways do you think Adam and Eve's actions affect your life each day?

Reminder: Scan this QR code to do the Meditation for this lesson and the Introduction for the next lesson:

Leader Guide

Objective: To describe the consequences of sin, identify the promise and provision of salvation in the context of Adam and Eve's sin, and analyze both how sin affects us today and how hope is possible in a world of sin

Response: Because Adam disobeyed God, we are separated from God and our only hope is in the promised Offspring.

Lesson Materials QR Code:

Review (10–15 minutes)

1. What are the different names or titles of God that you have seen in the passages from Lesson 1?
   *Note: Refer to the **Names of God Chart** in Lesson Materials.
   - **God:** The only true God, Creator, and Judge who is separate from everything else and better than everything else
   - **Lord:** The name of God that expresses a close relationship. In verse 4, we see that the Lord cares for mankind in a personal way. Also, in Genesis 1, we see that the Lord made mankind in His image. Because mankind was created in the image of God, mankind had a personal relationship with God as Lord.
   - **Lord:** The name of God that expresses ruling authority over us. We see God's lordship in His authority to create mankind in the way that He decides is good. We see God's authority when God gives directions to mankind and gives mankind the power to rule the earth.

2. What is God's relationship to mankind and what is man's relationship to God? What was the relationship like between God and mankind?
   - God is the creator of mankind, who made mankind to live in close relationship with Him under His rule as King.
   - Mankind is a creature who is made in God's image (Genesis 1:26–27) who has been given authority to rule, glory, and honor (Psalm 8:5–6).

- The relationship between God and mankind was good. God called His creation of mankind *very good*.

3. How does being made in the image of God influence how you understand God, yourself, and your purpose in life?
   - I understand God to be the creator of mankind, who made mankind to live in close relationship with Him under His rule as King.
   - Because I am made in the image of God, I have honor and glory. I am called to represent who God is by looking like Him in how I live.
   - Being created in the image of God means that I represent God by ruling over creation under God as His king. I am given a special purpose to rule the world according to God's laws and to seek to make my character look like the character of God.

4. What were the two trees called in the middle of the garden? What command did God give to the man about one of the trees? What would happen if man disobeyed God's command?
   - The two trees were the tree of life and the tree of the knowledge of good and evil.
   - He commanded Adam not to eat of the tree of the knowledge of good and evil.
   - Mankind would die.

5. How was the Garden of Eden the kingdom of God?
   - Definition for the kingdom of God: God's rule through God's people over God's place (adapted from Treat 2019).
     - God created mankind in His image to be rulers and blessed them with a close relationship with God, each other, and creation. He commanded mankind to subdue the earth and fill the earth so that the earth submits to God's rule.
     - God crowned Adam as the first son of man. He gave Adam the law of the kingdom. God set up Adam as the caretaker and guardian of Eden.
     - God established peace, creativity, family, work, etc.
     - The garden of Eden was the ideal, perfect place.
   - What did they *not* experience in the garden?
     - They did not experience shame, fear, death, conflict, pain, etc.

Introduction (5 minutes): Refer to the lesson.

Lesson Activity: Use the notes under Parts I, II, and III to fill out the **Sin and Sacrifice Mind Map** as you go through each part. Refer to the mind map in the lesson activity. In addition, there is a filled-in mind map in Lesson Materials: Additional Resources.

Lesson 2 (60 minutes)

Part I: Disobeying the Law of God (Genesis 3:1–7)
*Note: Refer to the **Sin and Sacrifice Mind Map** under lesson activity and begin filling in each part together as you learn additional information. For example, write *disobedience* in bubble 1 and *guilt* in bubble 2 because disobedience causes guilt.

1. What question did the serpent ask? What do you think was the intention behind this question? (v. 1)
   - "Did God really say, 'You must not eat from any tree in the garden'?"
   - The intention was to create doubt in the woman's mind and question God's reason in creating the law.

2. What did the snake tell the woman to convince her it was OK to disobey what God commanded? (v. 4)
   - You will not die; you will be wise; you will be like God …

3. What did the woman think of the fruit from the tree of the knowledge of good and evil? (v. 6)
   - It was good for food, desirable, and would make her wise.
   - What are some things that feel good but are bad for us?
     ❖ Consider how things appear or seem; for example, taking revenge on someone for hurting me feels good but is wrong.

Part II: Consequences of Guilt (Genesis 3:8–19)
*Note: Continue filling in the **Sin and Sacrifice Mind Map** as you learn additional information. For example, write *shame* in bubble 3, *fear* in bubble 4, and *brokenness* in bubble 5 because shame, fear, and brokenness are consequences of guilt.

1. What did the man and his wife hear? What does that say about the relationship God had and wanted to have with mankind? (v. 8)
   - The sound of the Lord God walking in the garden
   - God wanted to spend time with mankind. He established a different relationship with them than he had with the rest of creation. God created mankind to be with Him in a close, personal relationship.

2. What did Adam and Eve do after they ate the fruit? (v. 8)
   - Covered themselves, hid, and blamed each other

3. What did they experience for the first time? (v. 10) *

   *Note: After identifying shame, fear, and brokenness, ask the sub-questions one by one.
   - **Shame:** Because they disobeyed God's law (did something wrong; committed a sin), they felt shame.
     - ❖ Definition of shame from Lesson 1: Loss of respect or honor; a feeling of embarrassment because you have done something wrong
     - ❖ What action showed that the man and his wife felt shame? The man and his wife tried to cover themselves with leaves because their eyes were opened to their nakedness and shame. When God created Adam and Eve, He blessed them with honor and glory. Their disobedience damaged their honor and diminished their glory. Instead of viewing their bodies with honor, they now viewed their bodies with dishonor. Sin brought dishonor to their bodies and changed their minds and hearts.
   - **Fear:** Because they disobeyed God's law, they were afraid of what might happen or the consequences of what they did wrong.
     - ❖ What action showed that the man and his wife felt fear? The man and woman hid because they were afraid of God's judgment for disobeying God's law.
   - **Brokenness:** Because they broke (disobeyed) God's law, their eyes were opened so that they could no longer have the same relationship or go back to the relationship they once had with each other, creation, and God.
     - ❖ What action showed that the man and his wife felt brokenness? They blamed someone else because they were guilty. To blame means to make someone else responsible for something that was wrong. Both the woman and the man were guilty of breaking God's law. Adam blamed the woman God put in the garden, and the woman blamed the serpent. They now knew they were naked, and they no longer had peace because the relationship between God and mankind had been broken.

4. How do we experience some of the same things as Adam and Eve?
   - Yes, when we sin, we also feel shame or fear. We might try to hide what we did because we are embarrassed, don't know what to do, or are afraid of what will happen.

5. What punishments did God give Adam and Eve? (vv. 14–19)
   - God punished the woman by making childbearing painful.
   - God cursed the ground so that man's work would be difficult.

6. What does returning to the ground in verse 19 mean?
   - Death: the body turns back into dust.
   - What did God say would happen if they disobeyed the law? *
     - ❖ "When you eat from it you will certainly die."
   - What did the serpent say would happen? *
     - ❖ Their eyes would be opened and they will be like God knowing good and evil.
   - What actually happened? *
     - ❖ Their eyes were opened, and they realized they were naked (had knowledge they previously didn't have). This new knowledge brought guilt, shame, and eventually death. Before Adam sinned, they only had knowledge of good because they were created in the image of God—good, and innocent. This new knowledge of evil corrupted the image of God in them and damaged the goodness they originally had. Even though they did not immediately die, God is saying they will now die and turn back into dust. The word of God was true, but the word of the snake was a lie.

Part III: Provision for Mankind (Genesis 3:20–24)
*Note: Continue filling in the **Sin and Sacrifice Mind Map** as you learn additional information. Write *covering* in bubble 6 and *Offspring* in bubble 7 because the promise of the covering through sacrifice and the Offspring to defeat sin and death are provisions for guilt.

1. Read verses 23–24. How did the relationship between God and Adam and Eve change? *
   - Before they disobeyed God, they only knew good. They walked in the presence of God. When their eyes were opened, they knew both good and evil. This was not something God wanted for people to experience. Because they disobeyed God's command, they now knew what evil was. Because they were corrupted by evil, the relationship between God and mankind was broken, and they were banished from God's close presence.
   - What came into the world for the first time?
     - ❖ Guilt through sin and death entered into God's perfect world. When people disobey God's law, we call it "sin."
     - ❖ Death is the loss of harmony and the experience of brokenness, shame, and fear in our relationships with God, mankind, and creation. Adam and Eve hid from God and blamed each other.
     - ❖ Death is the state of being removed from God's blessing and placed under His curse because of the broken relationship between God and mankind.

- How do we know Adam and Eve were guilty from the passage?
  - ❖ We know Adam and Eve were guilty because they broke the law of God in the Garden of Eden and experienced the judgment of God.
  - ❖ God, the creator of both Adam and Eve, is the giver of the law. As Creator, He has the right to establish the law and pronounce punishments for mankind when it is broken. When Adam and Eve broke the law, they became sinners under the judgment of God. As a just judge, He must follow through with the punishments. Because God cannot live with sin, He banished Adam and Eve from His presence in the Garden of Eden and from the tree of life, a symbol of eternal life, to exist in a cursed world, resulting in eventual physical death.
- **Digging Deeper:** How does Adam's guilt affect us today?

  *Note: Refer to the **Image of God Chart** as a visual to show how Adam had corrupted the image of God in mankind. The glory and honor God had given mankind through Adam when He created man and woman in His own image was now corrupted, resulting in mankind rebelling against God's rule and purpose for them in this world and falling under the judgment of death.
  - ❖ As the first son of man figure, Adam was given a special place of authority over all of creation as God's representative. When Adam disobeyed, the consequences of his guilt came on all of mankind because he was mankind's representative.

Section Recap: Use the statement below to give learners a brief summary of terms:
Sin and Sacrifice Mind Map

Disobedience to the law of God is sin. When someone sins, they become guilty. All humanity is guilty of sin. The consequences/results of this guilt are shame, fear, and brokenness.

---

2. Read verse 21. What did God provide for Adam and Eve? Does He still care for them? *
   - God provided clothes for them, showing that He still cared for them.
     - ❖ Provision(n); provide(v): The act of giving something to someone to take care of their needs
   - What were the clothes made of? What do you think this means? (v. 21)

     *Note: The full explanation comes in Isaiah 53 in Lesson 8. This is the beginning of the sacrifice narrative that culminates in Isaiah 53.

- The garments were made of skin, which means animals had to be sacrificed to cover Adam and Eve's shame, and blood had to be spilled to remove their guilt. This symbolized the removal of their guilt and the covering of their nakedness and shame.

3. Read verse 15. What is the relationship between the woman's Offspring and the serpent? *
   - The woman's Offspring and the snake are enemies.
   - What do they do to each other?
     - The snake strikes the heel of the woman's Offspring, and the woman's Offspring crushes the head of the snake.
   - What hope does God give to mankind?
     - In the end, the Offspring of the woman will be victorious because He will crush the head of the snake. The snake uses sin to bring death to mankind. The Offspring will destroy the snake by defeating sin and death. In the coming weeks we will see how this happens!

Section Recap: Use the statements below to give learners a brief summary of terms:
Sin and Sacrifice Mind Map

God will provide a covering for shame and guilt through sacrifice and the Offspring of the woman who will have victory over the snake and sin and death.

Overarching Themes: Refer to the lesson.
*Note: Genesis 3:15 and 3:21 provide the structure for the study as we trace these two themes through the Old and New Testament.

Wrap-up (10–15 minutes)

- Ask learners: What is the purpose of the lesson?
  - To understand the consequences of disobeying God's command and how we can have hope in a world of sin and death
- Ask learners: What is one new thing that you learned today?
- State to learners: Think about this **Key Lesson Question:**
  - In what ways do you think Adam and Eve's actions affect your life each day?

LESSON 3
Kingdom Exile

Review

1. In the beginning of creation, what was the relationship like between God and mankind in the Garden of Eden (the kingdom of God)?
2. What happened to the relationship between God and mankind?
3. In what ways do you think Adam and Eve's actions affect your life each day?
4. What is the relationship between the woman's Offspring and the serpent?
   - What do they do to each other?
   - What hope does God give to mankind?

Introduction

Purpose: To understand that all mankind is sinful from the heart and can only be saved through faith in the Word of God

Lesson Context: Adam and Eve turned from their sin and began to trust in the Lord. Adam and Eve began having children and filling the earth as God commanded them to. Sadly, the sin of Adam continued in his family. His firstborn son, Cain, followed the evil of the snake, and killed his brother, Abel. Despite the continued sin, God blessed Adam and Eve with another son, Seth. The family of Seth "began to call upon the name of the Lord." The lineage of the promised Offspring who would defeat sin and death had begun!

Vocabulary

- Anger of God: God's response to sin that is consistent with the purity of His character and comes out of His righteous rule over His creation

- Burnt offering: An animal sacrifice which symbolized the removal of guilt by the animal dying in the place of the sinner to restore a right relationship with God

- Call upon the name of the Lord: To come in faith to the Lord for salvation from God's anger through the sacrifice that removes sinners' guilt and covers their shame so that they are restored to relationship with God as their Lord

- Heart: The part inside the person that controls how one thinks, desires, and feels
- Paradise: The restored (greater) Garden of Eden where God's people live in God's presence to experience the fullness of His blessing (great beauty, harmony, and peace)
- Regret (God as subject): To feel great sadness toward someone
- Save/Salvation: The act of God rescuing sinners from His righteous anger
- Sheol: The place of God's judgment after the death of the physical body where the souls of sinners are separated from His blessing to experience His anger and be punished under His curse with fire

Part I: Sin of Mankind (Genesis 6:5–10)

The LORD saw how great the wickedness of humans had become on the earth, and that every inclination of the thoughts of the human heart was only evil all the time. ⁶ The LORD regretted that he had made human beings on the earth, and his heart was deeply troubled. ⁷ So the LORD said, "I will wipe from the face of the earth the human race I have created—and with them the animals, the birds and the creatures that move along the ground—for I regret that I have made them." ⁸ But Noah found favor in the eyes of the LORD. ⁹ This is the account of Noah and his family. Noah was a righteous man, blameless among the people of his time, and he walked faithfully with God. ¹⁰ Noah had three sons: Shem, Ham, and Japheth.

Discussion

1. What has mankind become like after Adam disobeyed? How has mankind become the offspring of the snake?
   - **Digging Deeper:** Adam is the first son of man who represented mankind to God. Instead of establishing God's rule over the earth, Adam disobeyed God's law. Because Adam sinned, all mankind has become sinners.

"And I will put enmity between you and the woman, and between your offspring and hers; he will crush your head, and you will strike his heel." (Genesis 3:15)

2. What was the LORD's response to mankind's sin? Why?
   - What does this say about God's character?

"Your eyes are too pure to look on evil; you cannot tolerate wrongdoing." (Habakkuk 1:13)

3. Who found favor with the LORD? Who was he?
   - What was Noah like in his heart?

"Seth also had a son, and he named him Enosh. At that time people began to call on the name of the Lord." (Genesis 4:26)

Part II: Salvation through Judgment (Genesis 6:11–14)

Now the earth was corrupt in God's sight and was full of violence. [12] God saw how corrupt the earth had become, for all the people on earth had corrupted their ways. [13] So God said to Noah, "I am going to put an end to all people, for the earth is filled with violence because of them. I am surely going to destroy both them and the earth. [14] So make yourself an ark of cypress wood…"

Genesis 7:1–7, 16

The LORD then said to Noah, "Go into the ark, you and your whole family, because I have found you righteous in this generation. [2] Take with you seven pairs of every kind of clean animal, a male and its mate, and one pair of every kind of unclean animal, a male and its mate, [3] and also seven pairs of every kind of bird, male and female, to keep their various kinds alive throughout the earth. [4] Seven days from now I will send rain on the earth for forty days and forty nights, and I will wipe from the face of the earth every living creature I have made." [5] And Noah did all that the LORD commanded him. [6] Noah was six hundred years old when the floodwaters came on the earth. [7] And Noah and his sons and his wife and his sons' wives entered the ark to escape the waters of the flood…[16] Then the LORD shut him in.

Genesis 7:11–12, 17–24

In the six hundredth year of Noah's life, on the seventeenth day of the second month—on that day all the springs of the great deep burst forth, and the floodgates of the heavens were opened. [12] And rain fell on the earth forty days and forty nights…[17] For forty days the flood kept coming on the earth, and as the waters increased they lifted the ark high above the earth. [18] The waters rose and increased greatly on the earth, and the ark floated on the surface of the water. [19] They rose greatly on the earth, and all the high mountains under the entire heavens were covered. [20] The waters rose and covered the mountains to a depth of more than fifteen cubits. [21] Every living thing that moved on land perished—birds, livestock, wild animals, all the creatures that swarm over the earth, and all mankind. [22] Everything on dry land that had the breath of life in its nostrils died. [23] Every living thing on the face of the earth was wiped out; people and animals and the creatures that move along the ground and the birds were wiped from the earth. Only Noah was left, and those with him in the ark. ²⁴ The waters flooded the earth for a hundred and fifty days.

Discussion

1. Read Genesis 6:13. What did God say He was going to do to the people of the earth? Why?
   - **Digging Deeper:** What did God say would happen if Adam and Eve disobeyed the law? What did the serpent say would happen? What happened?

Breakout Pivot: Image of God Chart

---

2. What was Noah's relationship to God? How did God save Noah?

3. What was mankind's relationship to God? How did God punish His enemies?
   - **Digging Deeper:** What does it mean to be banished from the kingdom of God after the death of the body?

"Behold, all souls are mine...the soul who sins shall die." (Ezekiel 18:4, ESV)

Paradise (Heaven)	Sheol (Hell)
Isaiah 51:3: The LORD will surely comfort Zion [God's people] and will look with compassion on all her ruins; he will make her deserts like Eden [Paradise], her wastelands like the garden of the LORD. Joy and gladness will be found in her, thanksgiving and the sound of singing.	**Deuteronomy 32:22, NKJV:** For a fire is kindled in My anger, and shall burn to the lowest hell.

Part III: Salvation through Sacrifice (Genesis 8:1, 13–17, 20–22)

But God remembered Noah and all the wild animals and the livestock that were with him in the ark, and he sent a wind over the earth, and the waters receded…¹³ By the first day of the first month of Noah's six hundred and first year, the water had dried up from the earth. Noah then removed the covering from the ark and saw that the surface of the ground was dry. ¹⁴ By the twenty-seventh day of the second month the earth was completely dry. ¹⁵ Then God said to Noah, ¹⁶ "Come out of the ark, you and your wife and your sons and their wives. ¹⁷ Bring out every kind of living creature that is with you—the birds, the animals, and all the creatures that move along the ground—so they can multiply on the earth and be fruitful and increase in number on it."

²⁰ Then Noah built an altar to the Lord and, taking some of all the clean animals and clean birds, he sacrificed burnt offerings on it. ²¹ The Lord smelled the pleasing aroma and said in his heart: "Never again will I curse the ground because of humans, even though every inclination of the human heart is evil from childhood. And never again will I destroy all living creatures, as I have done. ²² As long as the earth endures, seedtime and harvest, cold and heat, summer and winter, day and night will never cease."

Discussion

1. In verse 1, God says He "remembered Noah." What does this say about God's relationship with Noah?

2. Read verses 20–21. What did Noah do after he, his family, and the animals left the ark?
   - Why did people need to offer a sacrifice?
   - **Digging Deeper:** How is this sacrifice connected to Genesis 3:21?

"The Lord God made garments of skin for Adam and his wife and clothed them."

3. Look at verse 21. How does the Lord describe the human heart? When does the human heart become sinful?

   > "Surely I was sinful at birth, sinful from the time
   > my mother conceived me." (Psalm 51:5)

4. How was Noah different from mankind that was judged?
   - **Digging Deeper:** In what specific ways did Noah trust God? How was Noah's response to God's word different from Adam and Eve's response to God's word in the garden?

5. What was the Lord's response to Noah's sacrifice?

Key Lesson Question: From the first three lessons, what do we learn about God's character? How does God punish sinners? How does God save sinners?

Reminder: Scan this QR code to do the Meditation for this lesson and the Introduction for the next lesson:

THE BIG STORY

Leader Guide

Objective: To diagnose the sinful human heart as the source of evil actions that is inherited through Adam's sin, recognize God as the righteous judge who punishes guilty sinners, and identify that the only way to escape His righteous anger is through faith in the sacrifice

Response: The only way to escape the righteous anger of God is through faith in the sacrifice.

Lesson Materials QR Code:

Review Activity (5–10 minutes): Refer to Lesson Materials.

Review (5–10 minutes)

1. In the beginning of creation, what was the relationship like between God and mankind in the Garden of Eden (the kingdom of God)?
    - They walked and talked with God, indicating a good relationship. The relationship was harmonious, peaceful, full of life (not death), fruitfulness, and obedience.
    - God created mankind in His image to be rulers and blessed them with a close relationship with God, each other, and creation. God commanded them to subdue the earth and fill the earth so that the earth submits to God's rule. He crowned Adam as the first son of man. He gave Adam the law of the kingdom and set up Adam as the caretaker and guardian of Eden.
    - God established peace, creativity, family, work, etc.
    - The kingdom of God: God's rule through God's people over God's place

2. What happened to the relationship between God and mankind?
    - The relationship between God and mankind was broken. Because of their guilt, God placed His judgment on Adam and Eve, causing

them to be banished from the presence of God in the garden and to eventually die.

3. In what ways do you think Adam and Eve's actions affect your life each day?
   - I too am guilty of breaking God's law. I experience brokenness, shame, and fear in my life. One day, I too will die.

4. What is the relationship between the woman's Offspring and the serpent?
   - The woman's Offspring and the snake are enemies.
   - What do they do to each other?
     ❖ The snake strikes the heel of the woman's Offspring and the woman's Offspring crushes the head of the snake.
   - What hope does God give to mankind?
     ❖ In the end, the Offspring of the woman will be victorious because He will crush the head of the snake. The snake uses sin to bring death to mankind. The Offspring will destroy the snake by defeating sin and death. In the coming weeks we will see how this happens!

Introduction (10 minutes): Refer to the lesson.

Lesson 3 (45–50 minutes)

Part I: Sin of Mankind (Genesis 6:5–10)

1. What has mankind become like after Adam disobeyed? How has mankind become the offspring of the snake? (v. 5) *
   *Note: Read Genesis 3:15 in the lesson.
   - Mankind has become wicked (filled with sin: to break God's law) from the heart. Their evil actions came from their sinful hearts (The part inside the person that controls how we think, desire, and feel). The inclinations of their hearts (The natural way people think and desire that forms them into the person they are) were filled with sin so that they sinned greatly before the LORD who made them.
   - Mankind has become enemies of God and aligned with the snake, following the way of evil.
   - **Digging Deeper:** Refer to the lesson.

2. What was the LORD's response to mankind's sin? Why? (v. 7) *
   *Note: Read Habakkuk 1:13 in the lesson.
   - The LORD felt regret, being greatly troubled in His spirit by mankind's sin. The LORD created mankind to be righteous and live in His presence in beauty, peace, and harmony. But now, mankind has

aligned themselves with the evil snake and made themselves enemies of God. God responded with great sadness because of His creation's wickedness and with righteous anger against sinners, declaring certain and complete judgment over the people of the earth because they joined with the enemy of God by breaking His law.
- **Think About It:** God does not feel regret like we do because God never makes mistakes. He is not admitting to fault. He is expressing great disappointment in mankind using human language. Greatly troubled helps describe what regret means in this context. Sometimes, God expresses His emotions, using words we can understand but with a different meaning when applied to God because God is holy, and we are sinners.
- What does this say about God's character? *
    - ❖ God is separate from sin. He is perfectly pure, totally without sin. God cannot allow sin to go unpunished because sin is the opposite of God's character. He is the righteous ruler who pours out His anger on His enemies in righteous judgment.

3. Who found favor with the Lord? Who was he? (v. 8)
    *Note: Read Genesis 4:26 in the lesson.
    - Noah was a descendant of Seth (Genesis 5:1–32), the family line who called on the name of the Lord. Noah was in the line that the promised Offspring would come from.
    - What was Noah like in his heart? (v. 9)
        - ❖ Noah was "blameless" and "righteous" because he had a heart of faith (trust in the Lord that results in obedience to the word of the Lord).

Part II: Salvation through Judgment (Genesis 6:11–14; 7:1–7, 16, 11–12, 17–24)

1. Read Genesis 6:13. What did God say He was going to do to the people of the earth? Why? *
    - In righteous anger, God was going to send a flood to destroy the whole earth to punish mankind for their sin. They were violent, acting out of hearts that were corrupted by sin. Instead of being filled with righteousness according to God's rule, the earth was filled with violence and destruction. God is pure and cannot allow sin to go unpunished. Mankind has corrupted the image with which God created him.

- **Digging Deeper:** What did God say would happen if Adam and Eve disobeyed the law? What did the serpent say would happen? What happened?
  - ❖ **God:** "Certainly die"
  - ❖ **Satan:** "Not certainly die"
  - ❖ **Reality:** Certain and complete death—God's word was true, and Satan's word was a lie.

Breakout Pivot: Image of God Chart (10–15 minutes)

- **Fill in the blank directions** (5 minutes): Separate learners into groups of two or three. Have them match the correct description of Image Corrupted with the corresponding Image Given by writing the correct letter in the blank spaces using the word bank. Bring them back together as one group to clarify the right answers.
- **Compare and contrast directions** (5–10 minutes): Have them discuss the questions below. Bring them back together as one group to clarify the right answers.
  - ❖ Because of Adam's sin, how does mankind corrupt his glory and honor?
    - Mankind represents himself and seeks his own glory and honor. He corrupts the good character God created him with. He destroys the innocence he was given and damages his character so that he is unclean and undesirable.
  - ❖ Because of Adam's sin, how does mankind corrupt his dominion over the earth?
    - Mankind abuses power and carries out his own rule on the earth.
  - ❖ Because of Adam's sin, how does mankind corrupt his fruitfulness?
    - Mankind kills and destroys. Instead of filling the earth with godly offspring, mankind fills the earth with violence.

2. What was Noah's relationship to God? How did God save Noah? *
   - Noah had a personal relationship with God as His Lord. God loved Noah. After revealing the coming destruction and commanding Noah to build an ark, God saved Noah and his family from the floodwaters, rescuing him from the anger of God. Noah rightly feared God's judgment and turned to God's provision of the ark to be saved (The act of God rescuing sinners from His righteous anger).

3. What was mankind's relationship to God? How did God punish His enemies?

   *Note: Read Ezekiel 18:4 in the lesson.
   - Mankind was the enemy of God. God destroyed them completely as He promised to do. Mankind died under the curse of God, being banished from the kingdom of God. Anger is part of God's character. As the righteous Lord over His creation, God delivers judgment by pouring out His anger on His enemies because they have wronged their Lord and Creator.
     - ❖ **Anger of God:** God's response to sin that is consistent with the purity of His character and comes out of His righteous rule over His creation
   - **Digging Deeper:** What does it mean to be banished from the kingdom of God after the death of the body?

   *Note: Read the verse box in the lesson. Refer to the definitions for Paradise and Sheol in the Vocabulary. In addition, Sheol is used in different contexts with various meanings in the Old Testament. Sometimes, Sheol is only referring to death in general. However, we are focusing on the context and meaning of Sheol that describes the place of God's punishment of his enemies.
     - ❖ God owns all souls because He is Lord and Creator of mankind. God created mankind to live forever in His presence. Because of sin, mankind was banished from the kingdom of God in the Garden of Eden. Because the soul exists forever, mankind will exist somewhere after his physical body dies.
     - ❖ The Old Testament teaches about two places souls will go after the body dies: Paradise or Sheol.

Part III: Salvation through Sacrifice (Genesis 8:1, 13–17, 20–22)

1. In verse 1, God says He "remembered Noah." What does this say about God's relationship with Noah? *
   - God had a personal relationship with Noah as the Lord. God does not forget His people but loves His people and saves them from the curse of death.

2. Read verses 20–21. What did Noah do after he, his family, and the animals left the ark?
   - Noah offered a burnt offering as a sacrifice to God.
   - Why did people need to offer a sacrifice?
     - ❖ Because of Adam's sin, all mankind are sinners and need a sacrifice to remove their guilt and take their punishment. Because Noah was a sinner too, he also needed a sacrifice for himself.
   - **Digging Deeper:** How is this sacrifice connected to Genesis 3:21?
   *Note: Read Genesis 3:21 in the lesson.
     - ❖ God offered the first sacrifice for sinners in Eden when He killed the animal and clothed Adam and Eve with its skins. This symbolized the removal of their guilt and the covering of their shame.

3. Look at verse 21. How does the Lord describe the human heart? When does the human heart become sinful?
   *Note: Read Psalm 51:5 in the lesson.
   - The Lord describes every inclination of the human heart as sinful from childhood (the time from birth to adulthood). Humans are sinful from birth. Sin is not merely what we do but also what we think, desire, and feel.

4. How was Noah different from mankind that was judged? *
   *Note: For those who think that Noah, as a prophet, was sinless, point them to Genesis 9:18–27 to read later for more understanding.
   - Even though Noah was sinful at birth like every human, he is described as "blameless," faithful, and righteous. Noah had a relationship with God as his Lord. He was different because he had a heart of faith. While mankind followed their sinful hearts, he recognized his sin and offered a burnt offering to remove his guilt and restore his relationship to God as his Lord.
   - Noah called on the name of the Lord: He came in faith to the Lord for salvation from God's anger through the sacrifice that symbolized the removal of his guilt and the covering of his shame so that he could be restored to relationship with God as His Lord.
   - **Digging Deeper:** In what specific ways did Noah trust God? How was Noah's response to God's word different from Adam and Eve's response to God's word in the garden?
     - ❖ During the days before the flood, God watered the earth from either streams that came up out of the ground or a mist (Genesis 2:5–6). This is the first mention of God sending rain on the earth. Likely, nobody had ever seen rain before and definitely not

a worldwide flood. Noah trusted that God would send a flood, even though it had likely never rained: (1) He had to trust God's word, even though he couldn't imagine or really know what was about to happen. (2) He waited in the ark seven days before God sent the rain (Genesis 7:4). He had to trust God's word, even when it wasn't fulfilled immediately. (3) He had to trust that God would hold the ark together as the waters destroyed the earth.

- ❖ Noah believed the word of God was true. He built the ark, walked into the ark, and stayed in the ark because he believed only God could save him from destruction. Eve believed the word of the snake instead of the word of God. She listened to lies and disobeyed the law of God. Adam listened to his wife instead of the word of God. Adam and Eve's unbelief resulted in their disobedience to God's law. Noah's faith in the word of God resulted in obedience to God's word.

5. What was the LORD's response to Noah's sacrifice? *
   - The LORD was pleased with Noah's sacrifice because it came from a heart of faith (Genesis 6:9) and promised to sustain the world by His power as long as the world exists. The sacrifice symbolized the turning away of God's anger and brought the blessing of God on Noah.

Wrap-up (5–10 minutes)

- Ask learners: What is the purpose of the lesson?
  - ➤ To understand that all mankind is sinful from the heart and can only be saved through faith in the Word of God
- Ask learners: What is one new thing that you learned today?
- State to learners: Think about this **Key Lesson Question:**
  - ➤ From the first three lessons, what do we learn about God's character? How does God punish sinners? How does God save sinners?

LESSON 4
Covenant Faith

Review

1. What happened to the relationship between God and mankind? What will happen to the enemies of God after their bodies die?
2. What hope does God give to mankind?
3. How was Noah saved from the righteous anger of God?
4. From the first three lessons, what do we learn about God's character? How does God punish sinners? How does God save sinners?

Introduction

Purpose: To understand how mankind receives righteousness through the special covenant God made with Abram

Context: After several generations we are introduced to a new man named Abram. (A generation is now roughly twenty to thirty years. It may have been a bit longer in Abram's day.) Abram was born and married a woman named Sarai in a place called Ur of the Chaldeans. Eventually, Abram, his wife, and other family members moved to a new place called Harran. We also learn that Sarai, Abram's wife, was barren and could not give birth to a child.

Vocabulary

- Believe: To put one's trust in the LORD
- Covenant: An unchangeable agreement that creates a unique relationship between God and man, includes promises and blessings, and requires punishment if the agreement is broken
- Credit: The act of God adding righteousness to a sinner's relational account with God
- Heir: The son who will have legal right to the possessions that belong to a relative when they die; one who will continue the family name
- LORD: The personal name of God that shows Him as the covenant-making and covenant-keeping God

- Lord/Sovereign: The name of God that shows Him as the King with complete *authority* who delivers His people from their enemies
- Righteousness: Right status before the Lord that is based on full obedience to His law and results in right relationship with the Lord (Bankston and Pierson 2019, 59)
- Sin debt: Something a person owes God because of their sin

Part I: Promise to Abram (Genesis 12:1–4, 6–8)

The Lord had said to Abram, "Go from your country, your people and your father's household to the *land* I will show you. ² I will make you into a *great nation*, and I will bless you; I will make your *name great*, and you will be a blessing. ³ I will bless those who bless you, and whoever curses you I will curse; and *all peoples on earth will be blessed through you.*"

⁴ So Abram went, as the Lord had told him … ⁶ Abram traveled through the land as far as the site of the great tree of Moreh at Shechem. At that time the Canaanites were in the land. ⁷ The Lord appeared to Abram and said, "To your offspring I will give this land." So he built an altar there to the Lord, who had appeared to him. ⁸ From there he went on toward the hills east of Bethel and pitched his tent, with Bethel on the west and Ai on the east. There he built an altar to the Lord and called on the name of the Lord.

Discussion

1. What did God tell Abram to do?
2. What promises did God give to Abram?
3. Read verses 6–8. How did Abram respond to God's promises to him (three actions)?
   - **Digging Deeper:** Both Noah and Abram "called on the name of the Lord." What does that mean?

Part II: Heir for Abram (Genesis 15:1–7)

The word of the Lord came to Abram in a vision: "Do not be afraid, Abram. I am your shield, your very great reward." ² But Abram said, "Sovereign Lord, what can you give me since I remain childless and the one who will inherit my estate is Eliezer of Damascus?" ³ And Abram said, "You have given me no children; so a servant in my household will be my heir." ⁴ Then the word of the Lord came to him: "This man will not be your heir, but a son who is your own flesh and blood will be your heir." ⁵ He took him outside and said, "Look up at the sky and count the stars—if indeed you can count them." Then he said to him, "So shall your offspring be."⁶ *Abram believed the* LORD, *and he credited it to him as righteousness.* ⁷ He also said to him, "I am the LORD, who brought you out of Ur of the Chaldeans to give you this land to take possession of it."

Discussion

1. How did God provide for (care for) Abram?
2. What was Abram's relationship to God?
3. Read verse 2. What was Abram's question to God? How does it connect to Genesis 12?
4. What was God's response to Abram's question? How does it connect to Genesis 12?
5. Read verse 6. How did Abram respond to God?
   - **Digging Deeper:** How was Abram's faith like Noah's faith?
   - God "credited it to him as righteousness." What does this mean?
6. How did Abram receive righteousness?
   - **Digging Deeper:** How did God describe Noah? How did Noah receive righteousness?

Part III: God's Covenant with Abram (Genesis 15:8–18)

But Abram said, "Sovereign LORD, how can I know that I will gain possession of it?" ⁹ So the LORD said to him, "Bring me a heifer, a goat and a ram, each three years old, along with a dove and a young pigeon." ¹⁰ Abram brought all these to him, cut them in two and arranged the halves opposite each other; the birds, however, he did not cut in half. ¹¹ Then birds of prey came down on the carcasses, but Abram drove them away.¹² As the sun was setting, Abram fell into a deep sleep, and a thick and dreadful darkness came over him. ¹³ Then the LORD said to him, "Know for certain that for four hundred years your descendants will be strangers in a country not their own and that they will be enslaved and mistreated there. ¹⁴ But I will punish the nation they serve as slaves, and afterward they will come out with great possessions.¹⁵ You, however, will go to your ancestors in peace and be buried at a good old age. ¹⁶ In the fourth generation your descendants will come back here, for the sin of the Amorites has not yet reached its full measure." ¹⁷ When the sun had set and darkness had fallen, a smoking firepot with a blazing torch appeared and passed between the pieces. ¹⁸ On that day the LORD made a covenant with Abram and said, "To your descendants I give this land, from the Wadi of Egypt to the great river, the Euphrates."

Discussion

1. Read verse 8. What was Abram's question?
2. How did God show He will keep His promise to Abram?
   - What is a covenant?

Breakout Pivot: Covenant Chart

---

3. Why was God making a covenant with Abram?
4. Did Abram do anything to deserve the covenant? Why or why not?

"Joshua said to all the people, 'This is what the Lord, the God of Israel, says: 'Long ago your ancestors, including Terah the father of Abram and Nahor, lived beyond the Euphrates River and worshiped other gods. But I took your father Abram from the land beyond the Euphrates and led him throughout Canaan and gave him many descendants.'" (Joshua 24:2–3)

Key Lesson Question: What does the covenant ceremony represent? What hope does God give to mankind through the covenant?

Reminder: Scan this QR code to do the Meditation for this lesson and the Introduction for the next lesson:

Leader Guide

Objective: To describe God's covenant with Abram as a gracious covenant and interpret Abram's faith as the only way to receive the righteousness of God

Response: Because of God's covenant promise, we can receive righteousness through faith in the Lord.

Lesson Materials QR Code:

Review Activity (5–10 minutes): Refer to Lesson Materials.

Review (5–10 minutes)

1. What happened to the relationship between God and mankind? What will happen to the enemies of God after their bodies die?
   - The relationship between God and mankind was broken. Because of their guilt, God placed His judgment on Adam and Eve, causing them to be banished from the presence of God in the garden and to eventually die.
   - Because mankind has corrupted God's image in them and become enemies through evil actions from a sinful heart, God will pour out His righteous anger on them. God will banish His enemies to Sheol: The place of God's judgment after the death of the physical body where the souls of sinners are separated from His blessing to experience His anger and be punished under His curse with fire.

2. What hope does God give to mankind?
   - In the end, the Offspring of the woman will be victorious because He will crush the head of the snake. The snake uses sin to bring death to mankind. The Offspring will destroy the snake by defeating sin and death. In the coming weeks we will see how this happens!

3. How was Noah saved from the righteous anger of God?
   - Noah was saved from the righteous anger of God through faith in the word of God. Noah came in faith to the Lord for salvation from God's anger through the sacrifice that symbolized the removal of his guilt and the covering of his shame so that he could be restored to relationship with God.

4. From the first three lessons, what do we learn about God's character? How does God punish sinners? How does God save sinners?
   - God is the righteous Lord over His creation who rules according to the perfection of His character. God is separate from sin. He is perfectly pure, totally without sin. God cannot allow sin to go unpunished because sin is the opposite of God's character.
   - As the righteous Lord over His creation, God punishes sinners by pouring out His anger on His enemies because they have wronged their Lord and Creator.
   - As the loving Lord who desires to have a personal relationship with mankind, God saves sinners by rescuing them from the anger of God so that they escape God's judgment. God saves sinners, like Noah, who call on the name of the Lord: to come in faith to the Lord for salvation from God's anger through the sacrifice that symbolized the removal of sinners' guilt and the covering of their shame so that they are restored to relationship with God as their Lord.

Introduction (10 minutes): Refer to the lesson.

Lesson 4 (45–50 minutes)

Part I: Promise to Abram (Genesis 12:1–4; 6–8)

1. What did God tell Abram to do? (v. 1)
   - God told Abram to leave his home and go to a land of promise.

2. What promises did God give to Abram? (vv. 2–3) *
   *Note: This will be the paradigm for the covenant promises that we will use from Adam to Jesus.
   - A great nation, a great name, a great blessing

3. Read verses 6–8. How did Abram respond to God's promises to him (three actions)?
   - Abram traveled to the land of promise, built an altar to the Lord, and "called on the name of the Lord."
   - **Digging Deeper:** Both Noah and Abram "called on the name of the Lord." What does that mean?
     - ❖ They came in faith to the Lord for salvation from God's anger and the just punishment of their sins through the sacrifice that symbolized the removal of their guilt and the covering of their shame to restore them to relationship with God as their Lord.

Part II: Heir for Abram (Genesis 15:1–7)

1. How did God provide for (care for) Abram? (vv. 1, 4–5)
   - He came to Abram and spoke to him in a vision.
   - He comforted Abram by promising protection ("Your shield").
   - He promised an heir (the line of the promised Offspring) and descendants. (vv. 4–5)

2. What was Abram's relationship to God? (vv. 1–2)
   *Note: Review the **Names of God Chart**. Then explain:
   - Abram, though a sinner, was restored to relationship with God as his Lord. He enjoyed a close, personal relationship with God where he lived under God's blessing. Abram called God Sovereign Lord. This indicates a personal relationship in which God is the King (Sovereign/Lord) and Abram is God's servant. Like Adam, God blessed Abram and gave him a special responsibility to bless all nations.

3. Read verse 2. What was Abram's question to God? How does it connect to Genesis 12?
   - Abram wanted to know who his heir would be because he had no children.
   - In Genesis 12:4, Abram was seventy-five years old when God told him all people groups would be blessed through him. Many years had passed, and Abram didn't understand how this would happen when his wife was barren. He had waited many years but still did not know how God would fulfill his promises to be a great nation, make his name great, and be a great blessing to every people group when he and his wife couldn't have children.

4. What was God's response to Abram's question? How does it connect to Genesis 12? (v. 4) *
   - God made it clear that Abram would have a biological child and that heir would bless all nations and grow into a great kingdom. He compared the number of offspring (descendants) to stars in the sky. The offspring of promise are those who believe the word of God. From the offspring of promise, there will be one Offspring who will defeat sin and death!
   - This heir of Abram will bless all nations. This is God restoring what was lost because of the curse by making Abram into a nation that would be a blessing to every people group on earth.

5. Read verse 6. How did Abram respond to God? *
   - Abram believed the Lord. He believed God even when he didn't fully understand how God would produce an heir when his wife was barren. He trusted God and chose to honor God by listening to God's word.
   - **Digging Deeper:** How was Abram's faith like Noah's faith?
     - Abram and Noah both believed the word of God, even when they couldn't fully understand what God's word meant, and there was a delay in the fulfillment of God's word. Noah believed God would send a flood of rain when rain had likely never happened before; Abram believed God's word, even though it was humanly impossible for his wife to have a child. Noah waited seven days; Abram had been waiting many years.
   - God "credited it to him as righteousness." What does this mean?
   *Note: Draw the **Relational Account Diagram** as you explain:
     - **Debit:** The record in a bank account of money that is owed to someone else
     - **Sin debt:** Money that is borrowed from someone else and must be paid back to the owner by a specific time; in this case, the payment for the debt is death. We call this our sin debt.
     - **Credit:** The action of one person putting money into another person's bank account; In this case, righteousness, not money, is being put into the account.
     - **Righteousness:** Right status before the Lord that is based on full obedience to His law and results in right relationship with the Lord (Bankston and Pierson 2019, 59)
     - **Summary:** Everyone has an account before God that shows the status of their relationship to God. We either have a sin debt or righteousness in our account.

6. How did Abram receive righteousness? (v. 6) *
   - Abram received righteousness through faith alone in the Lord. Abram, like all mankind, was born with an account full of sin as an enemy of God. We call it the sin debt. When Abram put his faith in the Lord, God replaced his sin debt with a credit of righteousness. Because of this righteousness that was given by the Lord, Abram was forgiven and accepted by God. Abram went from being an enemy of God to being restored to relationship with God as his Lord through faith alone.
   - **Digging Deeper:** How did God describe Noah? How did Noah receive righteousness?
       - ❖ God described Noah as "righteous." Noah received righteousness through faith in the Lord, just like Abram did. Both Noah and Abram were born sinners, like all mankind, and enemies of God through Adam's sin. However, they were restored to relationship with God as their Lord by calling on the name of the Lord: They came in faith to the Lord for salvation from God's anger through the sacrifice that symbolized the removal of their guilt and the covering of their shame so that they could be restored to relationship with God as their Lord. Only those who have been restored to relationship with God through faith alone have righteousness.

Part III: God's Covenant with Abram (Genesis 15:8–18)

1. Read verse 8. What was Abram's question?
   - Abram wanted assurance that God would keep His promise.

2. How did God show He will keep His promise to Abram? (v. 18) *
   - God made a covenant with Abram.
   - What is a covenant? A covenant is an unchangeable agreement that creates a unique relationship between God and man, includes promises and blessings, and requires punishment if the agreement is broken.
       - ❖ What are the promises and blessings? Great name, great nation, and great blessing to all nations
       - ❖ What is the punishment and curse for failing to keep the covenant? Death
       - ❖ The covenant is more than a promise because it creates a unique relationship between God and Abram. Like two people who enter a marriage covenant together, a man and a woman have a unique relationship in which they make promises to each other but also are bonded together in a special way.

- Leader Explains: The covenant ceremony symbolized the making of a formal, permanent relationship.
  - ❖ God represented Himself through "a smoking firepot with a blazing torch" (v. 17). The action of God symbolically passing in between the pieces (v. 17) established the relationship. Normally, both groups/people who made a covenant together would walk through the pieces together. This symbolized that the one who breaks the covenant will die, like the animals. By walking through the pieces alone, God promised that He will do what He has promised by Himself. The other person in the relationship, Abram, was sleeping. This is also the first indication that God will take the curse on Himself in the place of sinners. While God cannot literally die as God, the Bible will eventually reveal the full significance of this symbol. We will learn more about this in future lessons.
  - ❖ The covenant relationship is one-sided because God promised to take the punishment if the covenant was broken either by Himself or by Abram. God was the one who established it and will keep the covenant because He is the LORD.

Breakout Pivot: Covenant Chart (5–10 minutes)

- **Fill in the blank directions:** Separate learners into groups of two or three. Have them fill in the chart by writing the correct letter in the blank spaces using the word bank. Bring them back together as one group to clarify the right answers.
  *Note: First, show them an example; then have them do it.
  - ❖ Learner 1: What is one of the blessings of the covenant with Adam?
  - ❖ Learner 2: God blessed Adam with a great name. He was given glory and honor.

3. Why was God making a covenant with Abram?
   - Abram was a man who was still sinful and affected by the curse we learned about in Genesis 3. God is restoring all nations to relationship with Him because the LORD desires to be in relationship with His people. Remember that God will bless every people group through the Offspring of Abram.

4. Did Abram do anything to deserve the covenant? Why or why not?
   *Note: Some people think that Abram was sinless. Emphasize how Abram was a sinner. Read Joshua 24:2–3 in the lesson.
   - Abram was a sinner, like everyone who comes from Adam, and he came from a family that worshiped idols.
     - ❖ While Abram is not mentioned directly as worshiping idols, it is said that his family worshiped idols. The passage connects "the land beyond the Euphrates" with idol worship. Thus, Abram coming from the land of idol worship implies he was part of it. That is why he needed to be removed to show his separation from his idol worshiping past.
   - God initiated the relationship with Abram through the covenant.
     - ❖ God came to Abram and called him out of idolatry.
   - Abram didn't work for the relationship. God promised to do what the covenant required.
     - ❖ The works of mankind only contribute to a greater sin debt. When someone works at a job, he deserves the reward for his work. However, Abram did not work for his righteousness. Instead, God walked through the pieces of the sacrifice by Himself *symbolizing* that He will do what the covenant requires and take the curse of the broken covenant. Because God will do the work for Abram, Abram doesn't deserve it. The covenant relationship is a gift from God that can only be received through faith in the Lord. The covenant is by grace alone through faith alone.
     - ❖ **Symbol:** A physical sign (event/word/action) that points to something (idea or spiritual truth) greater or someone greater

Wrap-up (5–10 minutes)

- Ask learners: What is the purpose of the lesson?
  - ➢ To understand how mankind receives righteousness through the special covenant God made with Abram
- Ask learners: What is one new thing that you learned today?
- State to learners: Think about this **Key Lesson Question:**
  - ➢ What does the covenant ceremony represent? What hope does God give to mankind through the covenant?

LESSON 5
Burnt Offering

Review

1. What was Abram's relationship to God?
2. How did Abram receive righteousness?
3. What does the covenant ceremony represent? What hope does God give to mankind through the covenant?
4. Why did Abram not deserve to have a relationship with God (two reasons)?

Introduction

Purpose: To understand why sacrifice is necessary and how it affects mankind's relationship with God

Context: In Genesis 16, we learn that Sarai gave her servant Hagar to Abram to produce a child to fulfill what God says. They had a son named Ishmael when Abram was eighty-six years old. In Genesis 17, God visited Abram and changed Abram's name to Abraham, which means "Father of many nations." Abraham was given a special responsibility and blessing to be the father of the nations in the kingdom of God. God also changed Sarai's name to Sarah, saying, "I will bless her and will surely give you a son by her. I will bless her so that she will be the mother of nations; kings of peoples will come from her" (Genesis 17:16). God says Sarah will have a son called Isaac. Isaac is the heir whom God will bless and keep His covenant with his descendants. In Genesis 21, God kept His promise and caused Sarah to give birth to Isaac, the covenant heir.

Vocabulary

- Altar: A pile of stones on which wood is placed to burn a sacrificed animal
- Descendants: A group of people that comes from a specific person
- Faith/Faithfully: Trust in the Lord that results in obedience to the word of the Lord
- Instead of/Substitution: Using something or someone in the place of another thing or person
- Worship: To give honor to God

Part I: Testing of Abraham (Genesis 22:1–5)

Sometime later God tested Abraham. He said to him, "Abraham!" "Here I am," he replied.² Then God said, "Take your son, your only son, whom you love—Isaac—and go to the region of Moriah. Sacrifice him there as a burnt offering on a mountain I will show you."³ Early the next morning Abraham got up and loaded his donkey. He took with him two of his servants and his son Isaac. When he had cut enough wood for the burnt offering, he set out for the place God had told him about.⁴ On the third day Abraham looked up and saw the place in the distance.⁵ He said to his servants, "Stay here with the donkey while I and the boy go over there. We will worship and then we will come back to you."

Discussion

1. From previous readings, what promises had God given to Abraham about his son?
2. What did God tell Abraham to do? Why?
3. Read verse 5. What do you think Abraham meant when he said, "we will come back to you"?
    - **Digging Deeper:** Read Hebrews 11:17–19, which records that Abraham believed God would raise Isaac from the dead.

"By faith Abraham, when God tested him, offered Isaac as a sacrifice. He who had embraced the promises was about to sacrifice his one and only son, even though God had said to him, 'It is through Isaac that your offspring will be reckoned.' Abraham reasoned that God could even raise the dead, and so in a manner of speaking he did receive Isaac back from death."

Part II: The Greater Sacrifice (Genesis 22:6–18)

Abraham took the wood for the burnt offering and placed it on his son Isaac, and he himself carried the fire and the knife. As the two of them went on together, ⁷ Isaac spoke up and said to his father Abraham, "Father?" "Yes, my son?" Abraham replied. "The fire and wood are here," Isaac said, "but where is the lamb for the burnt offering?" ⁸ Abraham answered, "God himself will provide the lamb for the burnt offering, my son." And the two of them went on together. ⁹ When they reached the place God had told him about, Abraham built an altar there and arranged the wood on it. He bound his son Isaac and laid him on the altar, on top of the wood. ¹⁰ Then he reached out his hand and took the knife to slay his son.
¹¹ But the angel of the Lord called out to him from heaven, "Abraham! Abraham!" "Here I am," he replied. ¹² "Do not lay a hand on the boy," he said.

"Do not do anything to him. Now I know that you fear God, because you have not withheld from me your son, your only son." ¹³ Abraham looked up and there in a thicket he saw a ram caught by its horns. He went over and took the ram and sacrificed it as a burnt offering instead of his son. ¹⁴ So Abraham called that place The Lord Will Provide. And to this day it is said, "On the mountain of the Lord it will be provided." ¹⁵ The angel of the Lord called to Abraham from heaven a second time ¹⁶ and said, "I swear by myself, declares the Lord, that because you have done this and have not withheld your son, your only son, ¹⁷ I will surely bless you and make your descendants as numerous as the stars in the sky and as the sand on the seashore. Your descendants will take possession of the cities of their enemies, ¹⁸ and through your offspring all nations on earth will be blessed, because you have obeyed me."

Discussion

1. Describe the main events of the story.
2. In what ways did Abraham show that he believed God? Why was this difficult for Abraham?
3. Why was a sacrifice necessary?
   - What punishment did Adam have because of his sin?
   - What has mankind become like after Adam disobeyed? What will happen to the enemies of God?

Breakout Pivot: Sacrifice Chart

---

4. Read verse 8. Abraham said, "God himself will provide the lamb for the burnt offering."
   - In the Garden of Eden, why did God kill the animal and clothe Adam and Eve?
   - Read verse 13. What did God provide as a sacrifice instead of Isaac?
   - Read verse 14. What is the symbolic meaning of the sacrifice?
   - **Digging Deeper:** How is this sacrifice connected to the sacrifice in the covenant ceremony?

"So the Lord said to him, 'Bring me a heifer, a goat and *a ram*, each three years old, along with a dove and a young pigeon.' Abram brought all these to him, *cut them* in two and arranged the halves opposite each other … When the sun had set and darkness had fallen, a smoking firepot with a blazing torch appeared and passed between the pieces. On that day the Lord made a covenant with Abram and said, 'To your descendants I give this land.'" (Genesis 15:9–10, 17–18)

5. Read verses 8 and 14. How is Abraham's righteousness connected to the future sacrifice?
   - **Digging Deeper:** Noah and Abraham came in faith to the Lord for salvation from God's anger through the sacrifice that symbolized the removal of their guilt and the covering of their shame so that they could be restored to relationship with God as their Lord. They put their faith, not in the animal sacrifice, but in the coming and greater Sacrifice.

6. Read verse 18. Who will bless all nations?
   - **Digging Deeper:** The covenant Offspring in Genesis 3, who will defeat the serpent and bless all nations, will be the Offspring of Abraham through His son, Isaac. Abraham is set up as a new Adam who is blessed by God and is given the promise of the kingdom of God through a covenant relationship. God is renewing His covenant relationship with mankind through Abraham by restarting a new humanity through Abraham's Offspring.

7. Why was Abraham blessed?
   - From this story, how was Abraham's obedience connected to his faith?
   - **Digging Deeper:** How is Genesis 22:18 connected to Genesis 15?

Genesis 15:6: Abram *believed* the Lord, and he credited it to him as righteousness.	**Genesis 22:18:** And through your offspring all nations on earth will be blessed, because you have *obeyed* me.

Key Lesson Question: How is it possible for sinners to receive righteousness and have a right relationship with God?

Reminder: Scan this QR code to do the Meditation for this lesson and the Introduction for the next lesson:

Leader Guide

Objective: To interpret Abraham's sacrifice of Isaac as a substitutionary sacrifice, analyze Abraham's sacrifice in light of the first sacrifice of Genesis 3:21, and articulate Abraham's relationship to God through his faith in the coming and greater Sacrifice

Response: To be restored to relationship with God, we must trust in the coming substitutionary Sacrifice.

Lesson Materials QR Code:

Review Activity (10–15 minutes): Refer to Lesson Materials.

Review (5–10 minutes)

1. What was Abram's relationship to God?
    - God initiated a covenant relationship with Abram. A covenant is an unchangeable agreement that creates a unique relationship between God and man, includes promises and blessings, and requires punishment if the agreement is broken.
        - ❖ Condition/Promise/Curse
    - Abram, though a sinner, was restored to relationship with God as his Lord. He enjoyed a close personal relationship with God where he lived under God's blessing. Abram called God Sovereign Lord. This indicates a personal relationship in which God is the King (Sovereign/Lord) and Abram is God's servant. Like Adam, God blessed Abram and gave him a special responsibility to bless all nations.

2. How did Abram receive righteousness?
    - Abram received righteousness through faith alone in the Lord. Abram, like all mankind, was born with an account full of sin as an enemy of God. We call it the sin debt. When Abram put his faith in the Lord, God replaced his sin debt with a credit of righteousness. Because of this righteousness that was given by the Lord, Abram was forgiven and accepted by God. Abram went from being an enemy of God to being restored to relationship with God as his Lord through faith alone.

3. What does the covenant ceremony represent? What hope does God give to mankind through the covenant?
   - The covenant ceremony symbolizes the making of a formal, permanent relationship. God represents Himself through "a smoking firepot with a blazing torch" (v. 17). The action of God symbolically passing in between the pieces (v. 17) establishes the relationship. Normally, both groups/people who make a covenant together will walk through the pieces together. This symbolizes that the one who breaks the covenant will die, like the animals. By walking through the pieces alone, God is saying that He will do what He has promised by Himself. The covenant relationship is one-sided because God promises to take the punishment if the covenant is broken either by Himself or by Abram. The other person in the relationship, Abram, was sleeping.
   - God promises to restore all nations to the kingdom of God through the covenant. This promise is dependent on God not us because it is a one-sided covenant. If we break the covenant, God Himself will take the curse for us. He will give us a great name, make us part of His great kingdom, and bless us through the promised Offspring of the woman who will defeat sin and death!

4. Why did Abram not deserve to have a relationship with God (two reasons)?
   - Abram was a sinner who came from worshiping idols.
   - Abram didn't work for the relationship. God promised to do what the covenant required.
     - ❖ When someone works at a job, he deserves the reward for his work. When God walked through the pieces of the sacrifice by Himself, He promised to do what the covenant requires or die like the animal. Because God will do the work for Abram, Abram didn't deserve it. The covenant relationship is a gift from God that can only be received through faith in the Lord. The covenant is by grace alone through faith alone.

Introduction (5 minutes): Refer to the lesson.

Lesson 5 (40–45 minutes)

Part I: Testing of Abraham (Genesis 22:1–5)

1. From previous readings, what promises had God given to Abraham about his son?
   - God makes it clear that Abraham would have a biological child and that heir would bless all nations and grow into a great kingdom. He

compares the number of the offspring of promise to stars in the sky. Isaac is the covenant heir from the offspring of promise. The covenant Offspring who will defeat the serpent will come from the line of the offspring of promise (Abraham through Isaac).
- This heir of Abraham, the covenant Offspring, will bless all nations. This is God restoring what was lost because of the curse by making Abraham into a nation that would be a blessing to every people group.

2. What did God tell Abraham to do? Why?
   - God told Abraham to sacrifice his only son as a burnt offering on Mount Moriah. According to verse 1, this was a test for Abraham. Would Abraham demonstrate his faith in God by obeying God or demonstrate a lack of faith in God by disobeying God?

3. Read verse 5. What do you think Abraham meant when he said, "we will come back to you"? *
   - While learners will probably have a variety of answers, this is evidence that Abraham believed God would do something to preserve Isaac, the covenant offspring.
   - **Digging Deeper:** Read Hebrews 11:17–19, which records that Abraham believed God would raise Isaac from the dead.
     *Note: Read Hebrews 11:17–19 in the lesson.

Part II: The Greater Sacrifice (Genesis 22:6–18)

1. Describe the main events of the story.
   - Abraham took Isaac, the wood, the fire, and the knife and built an altar.
   - He placed Isaac on the altar and went to strike his son.
   - Then, the angel of the Lord called out and stopped Abraham, and the Lord provided Abraham a ram to sacrifice instead of his son.
   - The Lord blessed Abraham and confirmed the covenant promise to Abraham.

2. In what ways did Abraham show that he believed God? Why was this difficult for Abraham?
   - Abraham was willing to obey God even to the point of offering his only son as a sacrifice. Abraham believed that he would see Isaac alive and return with Isaac and that God would provide a lamb.

3. Why was a sacrifice necessary? *
   - A sacrifice was necessary because the relationship between God and mankind had been broken.

- What punishment did Adam have because of his sin?
    - ❖ He was banished from the garden and presence of God. It also meant Adam and Eve would die.
    - ❖ This also affects all the descendants of Adam because Adam represented all mankind as the son of man. Because of Adam's guilt, God placed His judgment on all mankind. All people are now banished from the presence of God in His kingdom and will eventually die.
    - ❖ As a descendant of Adam, Abraham was also a sinner and deserved to die.
- What has mankind become like after Adam disobeyed? What will happen to the enemies of God?
    - ❖ Mankind has become wicked from the heart (The part inside the person that controls how we think, desire, and feel). Their evil actions came from their sinful hearts. The inclinations of their hearts (The natural way people think and desire that forms them into the person they are) were filled with sin so that they corrupted the image of God in them. Mankind has become enemies of God and aligned with the snake, following the way of evil.
    - ❖ God will pour out His righteous anger on them. God will banish His enemies to Sheol: The place of God's judgment after the death of the physical body where the souls of sinners are separated from His blessing to experience His anger and be punished under His curse with fire.

Breakout Pivot: Sacrifice Chart (5 minutes)

- **Matching Directions:** Separate learners into groups of two or three. Have them match the correct offering with its symbolism in the **Sacrifice Chart** by writing the correct letter and number under the correct sacrifice in the Matching Table. Bring them back together as one group to clarify the right answers.
    - ❖ Learner 1: What was sacrificed in the first sacrifice?
    - ❖ Learner 2: An animal (2) was sacrificed in the first sacrifice.
    - ❖ Learner 2: What did the sacrifice symbolize?
    - ❖ Learner 1: The sacrifice symbolized the greater Sacrifice who will remove guilt through the spilled blood and cover shame (A).

4. Read verse 8. Abraham said, "God himself will provide the lamb for the burnt offering." *
   - In the Garden of Eden, why did God kill the animal and clothe Adam and Eve?
     - ❖ Because of their sin, they deserved death. God killed the animal and clothed Adam and Eve to symbolize the covering of their shame with the skins of the animal and the removal of their guilt through its spilled blood.
   - Read verse 13. What did God provide as a sacrifice instead of Isaac?
     - ❖ God provided a ram as a sacrifice instead of Isaac.
   - Read verse 14. What is the symbolic meaning of the sacrifice?
     - ❖ Mankind needs his guilt removed and his shame covered through the blood of the sacrifice. The sacrifice died in the place of the sinner and restored man's relationship to God by removing guilt and making man acceptable to God.
     - ❖ It was said, "On the mountain of the Lord it will be provided" (v. 14). The grammar is in the future tense, meaning the animal sacrifice is a symbol that points to the greater Sacrifice who will come later.
       - **Symbol:** A physical sign (event/word/action) that points to something (idea or spiritual truth) greater or someone greater
     - ❖ This verse hints that there is a coming and greater Sacrifice who will restore sinners' relationship to God. Through this sacrifice, God will provide the debt payment for sin and remove guilt from His people.
   - **Digging Deeper:** How is this sacrifice connected to the sacrifice in the covenant ceremony?
     *Note: Read Genesis 15:9–10, 17–18 in the lesson.
     - ❖ In both places, a ram is used, and the animal is cut up for sacrifice. Remember the covenant ceremony, how God walked through the pieces of the sacrifice alone. God promised to take the curse of the covenant. Now, God himself provides a sacrifice that points to a greater Sacrifice who will take the covenant curse and die in place of the sinner.

5. Read verses 8 and 14. How is Abraham's righteousness connected to the future sacrifice? *
   *Note: Ask the following questions to fill out the **Relational Account Diagram** together: What is the debit? What is the credit? How do we go from a sin debt to a credit of righteousness? Then add the new piece that we receive righteousness through faith alone **in the greater Sacrifice**.

- Abraham received righteousness through faith in the greater Sacrifice who will remove his guilt through the spilled blood and cover his shame with righteousness.
- **Digging Deeper:** Refer to the lesson.

6. Read verse 18. Who will bless all nations? *
   - The Offspring [this word is singular] will bless all nations just as God promised in Genesis 12:1–3. The Offspring will restore all nations to the kingdom of God.
   - **Digging Deeper:** Refer to the lesson.
   *Note: Refer to the **Covenant Family Tree** in the Learner Guide.

7. Why was Abraham blessed? (v. 18) *
   - Abraham was blessed because he obeyed the word of the Lord.
   - From this story, how was Abraham's obedience connected to his faith?
     ❖ Abram's response of humble obedience was a result of his faith in the Lord. In verse 5, we learned that Abraham believed that he would see Isaac alive and return with Isaac. According to verse 10, Abraham obeyed out of a heart of faith that worshiped God. In verses 8 and 14, we learn that Abraham trusted that the Lord God would provide a lamb. Faith produces the response of obedience.
   - **Digging Deeper:** How is Genesis 22:18 connected to Genesis 15?
     *Note: Read the verse chart in the lesson as you explain. Remind learners that we do not obey God to have a relationship with God. We are given righteousness through faith in the Lord.
     ❖ First, Abraham believed the word of the Lord (Genesis 15:6). Second, Abraham obeyed the word of the Lord (Genesis 22:18). God confirmed His covenant with all its blessings in the covenant ceremony, in which God walked through the animals alone (Genesis 15:9–20). The promises were confirmed by God alone and given to Abraham through faith alone (Genesis 15:6).
     ❖ In addition, the promises of God (Genesis 12:1–3) always came before Abraham's obedience (Genesis 12:4; 17).

Wrap-up (10–15 minutes)

- Ask learners: What is the purpose of the lesson?
  - ➢ To understand why sacrifice is necessary and how it affects mankind's relationship with God
- Ask learners: What is one new thing that you learned today?
- State to learners: Think about this **Key Lesson Question:**
  - ➢ How is it possible for sinners to receive righteousness and have a right relationship with God?

LESSON 6
Kingdom Law Explained

Review

1. What is the punishment for sin/the cost of sin?

2. Abraham said, "God himself will provide the lamb for the burnt offering." (Genesis 22:8)
   - In the Garden of Eden, why did God kill the animal and clothe Adam and Eve?
   - What did God provide as a sacrifice instead of Isaac? What was the symbolic meaning of the sacrifice?

3. How is it possible for sinners to receive righteousness and have a right relationship with God (Genesis 15:6)?

4. How was the Garden of Eden a description of the kingdom of God?

5. What kind of relationship did Abraham have with the Lord? What promises did God give to Abraham? How are the promises connected to the kingdom of God?

Introduction

Purpose: To understand the law of God and what happens if mankind obeys or disobeys His commands

Context: Isaac had two sons, Jacob and Esau. God continued the covenant line through Jacob and his twelve sons. Just as God renamed Abram to Abraham, He renamed Jacob to Israel. The twelve sons who came from Israel are the twelve tribes of Israel. Israel traveled to Egypt and became "exceedingly fruitful; they multiplied greatly, increased in numbers and became so numerous that the land was filled with them" (Exodus 1:7). The Egyptian king became afraid of Israel and enslaved them. In Egypt, the people of Israel cried for help. God sent the prophet Moses to Egypt to save His people. God led the Israelites out of Egypt and through the Red Sea. Next, they traveled into the wilderness of Shur. Finally, they arrived at Mount Sinai three months after leaving Egypt.

Exodus Context: Exodus is the second book in the Bible, which was also written by Moses, and continues to tell the history of the Israelites and gives more details about God's relationship with Israel as His covenant people.

Vocabulary

- Ten Commandments: The law of God that describes the unchanging character of God
- Holy: Set apart for a special purpose; pure
- Jealous (God as subject): Extremely protective of someone or something for the good of that person or thing

Part I: The Old Covenant (Exodus 19:1–6)

On the first day of the third month after the Israelites left Egypt—on that very day—they came to the Desert of Sinai ... Israel camped there in the desert in front of the mountain. ³ Then Moses went up to God, and the Lord called to him from the mountain and said, This is what you are to say to the descendants of Jacob and what you are to tell the people of Israel...⁵ Now if you obey me fully and keep my covenant, then out of all nations you will be my treasured possession. Although the whole earth is mine, ⁶ you will be for me a kingdom of priests and a holy nation. These are the words you are to speak to the Israelites.

Discussion

1. Read Exodus 19:5–6. What relationship did God make with Israel?
   - What did God require Israel to do as the condition of the covenant?
   - What did God promise Israel?

Part II: The Ten Commandments (Exodus 20:1–17)

And God spoke all these words: ² "I am the Lord your God, who brought you out of Egypt, out of the land of slavery. ³ You shall have no other gods before me. ⁴ You shall not make for yourself an image in the form of anything in heaven above or on the earth beneath or in the waters below. ⁵ You shall not bow down to them or worship them; for I, the Lord your God, am a jealous God, punishing the children for the sin of the parents to the third and fourth generation of those who hate me, ⁶ but showing love to a thousand generations of those who love me and keep my commandments.
⁷"You shall not misuse the name of the Lord your God, for the Lord will not hold anyone guiltless who misuses his name."
⁸"Remember the Sabbath day by keeping it holy. ⁹ Six days you shall labor and do all your work, ¹⁰ but the seventh day is a sabbath to the Lord your God. On it you shall not do any work...¹¹ For in six days the Lord made the heavens and the

earth, the sea, and all that is in them, but he rested on the seventh day. Therefore, the Lord blessed the Sabbath day and made it holy."

¹² "Honor your father and your mother, so that you may live long in the land the Lord your God is giving you."

¹³ "You shall not murder. ¹⁴ You shall not commit adultery. ¹⁵ You shall not steal."

¹⁶ "You shall not give false testimony against your neighbor."

¹⁷ "You shall not covet your neighbor's house … or anything that belongs to your neighbor."

Discussion

1. Read Exodus 20:2. Who does God say He is?
2. List the Ten Commandments.

"Love...God with All Your Heart." (Deuteronomy 6:4-5)	Sin of the Heart towards God
1. You shall have no other _____.	
2. You shall not make an _____ or _____ down to an image of anything in heaven or on earth.	
3. You shall not misuse the _____ of the Lord.	
4. vRemember the _____ day by keeping it holy.	
"Love Your Neighbor as Yourself." (Leviticus 19:18)	**Sin of the Heart towards Man**
5. _____ your father and your mother.	
6. You shall not _____.	
7. You shall not commit _____.	
8. You shall not _____.	
9. You shall not bear _____ testimony against your neighbor.	
10. You shall not _____.	

- **Digging Deeper:** Remember how the Lord described the human heart: "Every inclination of the human heart is evil from childhood" (Genesis 8:21). Sin is not merely what we do but also what we think, desire, and feel.

Deuteronomy Context: Deuteronomy means the second law. It is the final book of the Torah. It focuses on the giving of the law and its application to the covenant people of Israel. It ends with the transition of leadership from Moses to Joshua and the renewing of the covenant between God and Israel. God was preparing His people to enter the land He had promised to Abraham and His descendants.

Part III: Covenant Blessing and Cursing (Deuteronomy 6:24–25)

The Lord commanded us to obey all these decrees and to fear the Lord our God, for our good always, that he might preserve us alive, as we are this day. ²⁵ And if we are careful to obey all this law before the Lord our God, as he has commanded us, that will be our righteousness.

Deuteronomy 11:26–28

See, I am setting before you today a blessing and a curse— ²⁷ the blessing if you obey the commands of the Lord your God that I am giving you today; ²⁸ the curse if you disobey the commands of the Lord your God and turn from the way that I command you today…

Deuteronomy 30:19

I call heaven and earth to witness against you today, that I have set before you life and death, blessing and curse.

Discussion

1. What are the decrees God commanded? How is the law good for the people of God?
2. What do we learn about the character of the Lord from His law?

Breakout Pivot: Kingdom through Covenant Chart

---

3. What would be the result if the people fully obeyed all the law of God?
   - Read Exodus 19:5–6. How does righteousness bring honor?
   - Read Deuteronomy 30:19. What is the blessing?

4. What would be the result if the people did not fully obey all the law of God?
   - Read Deuteronomy 11:28. How does unrighteousness bring shame?
   - Read Deuteronomy 30:19. What is the curse?

5. Is it possible for a person to fully obey all the law of God (follow all these laws all the time)?

"Every inclination of the human heart is evil from childhood." (Gen 8:21)

Key Lesson Question: What do you think will happen to you if you do not fully obey all the law of God?

Reminder: Scan this QR code to do the Meditation for this lesson and the Introduction for the next lesson:

THE BIG STORY

Leader Guide

Objective: To describe the relationship between God and Israel, understand some of the purposes of the Ten Commandments, and recognize people's inability to fulfill the requirements of the law to have a relationship with God

Response: We cannot obey God's commandments enough to maintain a relationship with Him.

Lesson Materials QR Code:

Review Activity (5–10 minutes): Refer to Lesson Materials.

Review (10–15 minutes)

1. What is the punishment for sin/the cost of sin?
    - Because of Adam's guilt, God placed His judgment on Adam and Eve, causing them to be banished from God's blessing in the garden and to eventually die. The cost of sin is the curse of death both physically and spiritually. God will pour out His righteous anger on His enemies in Sheol: The place of God's judgment after the death of the physical body where the souls of sinners are separated from His blessing to experience His anger and be punished under His curse with fire.

2. Abraham said, "God himself will provide the lamb for the burnt offering." (Genesis 22:8)
    - In the Garden of Eden, why did God kill the animal and clothe Adam and Eve?
        - ❖ Because of their sin, they deserved death. God killed the animal and clothed Adam and Eve to cover their shame with the skins of the animal and to remove their guilt through its spilled blood.
    - What did God provide as a sacrifice instead of Isaac? What was the symbolic meaning of the sacrifice?
        - ❖ God provided a ram as a sacrifice instead of Abraham's son.

- ❖ Mankind needs his guilt removed and his shame covered through the blood of the sacrifice. The sacrifice died in the place of the sinner, symbolizing the restoration of man's relationship to God through the greater Sacrifice who will remove guilt and make man acceptable to God.

3. How is it possible for sinners to receive righteousness and have a right relationship with God (Genesis 15:6)?
   - Abraham believed not only in the promises of God but also specifically in the coming and greater Sacrifice. Abraham believed that through the blood of the coming Sacrifice, his guilt was removed and his shame covered. Abraham received righteousness through faith alone in the coming Sacrifice.
   - Sinners must trust in God's sacrifice in their place to remove their guilt, not in their own ability to obey God or in their own attempts to earn back God's blessing or make amends for their sin.

4. How was the Garden of Eden a description of the kingdom of God?
   - In Eden, God ruled over His creation through Adam and Eve. God gave Adam the law of God and the responsibility to rule God's kingdom by taking care of it and guarding it. Adam and Eve were God's people. The land of Eden was the place of God's presence. God lived with His people in close relationship to them as their Lord.

5. What kind of relationship did Abraham have with the Lord? What promises did God give to Abraham? How are the promises connected to the kingdom of God?
   - God initiated or chose to have a covenant relationship with Abraham and Abraham's offspring through Isaac. This covenant created a unique relationship between God and His people, included promises and blessings, and required punishment if the agreement was broken.
   - God promised Abraham a great name, a great nation, and a great blessing. The Offspring (singular) would bless all nations. The great name, nation, and blessing to all people groups describes the kingdom of God as God seeks to restore His people from all tribes, make them into a great nation, and provide for them a land under His rule through the promised Offspring. God promises to restore His rule through His people over His place.

Introduction (10 minutes): Refer to the lesson.

Lesson 6 (40–45 minutes)

Part I: The Old Covenant (Exodus 19:1–6)

1. Read Exodus 19:5–6. What relationship did God make with Israel?
   - God made a covenant relationship with Israel. The Bible calls this covenant the old covenant.
   - What did God require Israel to do as the condition of the covenant?
     - ❖ God required the people to obey God fully. The covenant was conditioned on Israel's full obedience to the law of God.
   - What did God promise Israel?
     - ❖ God promised to make Israel a "treasured possession," a "kingdom of priests," and a "holy nation."

Part II: The Ten Commandments (Exodus 20:1–17)

1. Read Exodus 20:2. Who does God say He is? *
   - God says He is the LORD: the *personal name* of God that shows Him as the covenant-making and *covenant-keeping* God.

2. List the Ten Commandments.
   *Note: As a group, fill in the blanks in the first column to list the Ten Commandments. Then, fill in the second column to show how sin comes from the heart. The goal is to show the connection of sinful desire and thought to sinful action. Only discuss some examples and keep moving through them at a fast pace. This should not take longer than ten minutes. The answer key is in Lesson Materials.
   - **Digging Deeper:** Refer to the lesson.

Deuteronomy Context: Refer to the lesson.

Part III: Covenant Blessing and Cursing (Deuteronomy 6:24–25, 11:26–28, 30:19)

1. What are the decrees God commanded? How is the law good for the people of God?
   - The decrees are the Ten Commandments (the law) God gave to the people of Israel.
   - The law is meant to preserve life. It is a guide for how to live in right relation to God.

2. What do we learn about the character of the Lord from His law?
   - We learn that He is *sovereign/ruler*. He requires that we live under His law.
   - We learn that He is *relational*. He desires to be in close relationship with us.
   - We learn that the Lord God is *holy*. He cannot live with sin.
   - We learn that He is *just*. He will punish sin.
   - We learn that He is *jealous* for the honor of His name. He will protect His honor.
   - We learn that He is *loving*. He provides us with work to be productive, with the Sabbath to rest, and with His law that we might know how to please Him.

Breakout Pivot: Kingdom through Covenant Chart (15 minutes)

- **Fill in the blank directions** (5 minutes): Separate learners into groups of two or three. Have them fill in the chart by writing the correct letter in the blank spaces using the word bank. Bring them back together as one group to clarify the right answers.
  - ❖ Learner 1: Where was the place of the kingdom of God?
  - ❖ Learner 2: The place of the kingdom of God was Canaan.
- **Compare and contrast directions** (5–10 minutes): Have them use the chart to discuss the questions below. Bring them back together as one group to clarify the right answers.
  - ❖ How is the great blessing of the old covenant like the great blessing of the covenant with Abraham?
    - The great blessing of the old covenant is the nation of Israel as a kingdom of priests. The great blessing of the covenant with Abraham is that his Offspring would bless all nations. Both the Offspring of Abraham and the nation of Israel were appointed by the Lord to bless all nations.
  - ❖ What is different between the covenant curse with Abraham and the covenant curse with Israel?
    - God promises to take the covenant curse of the covenant with Abraham. However, God requires Israel to keep the covenant and take the curse of the covenant if they break the covenant.

3. What would be the result if the people fully obeyed all the law of God? *
   - If Israel obeyed the law of God, they would be righteous.
     - ❖ Righteousness: Right status before the Lord that is based on full obedience to His law and results in right relationship with the Lord (Bankston and Pierson 2019, 59)
   - Read Exodus 19:5–6. How does righteousness bring honor?
     - ❖ Righteousness results in the honor of being "a treasured possession." God offered to restore to Israel the honor that was corrupted by Adam's disobedience on the condition that they fully obey the law of God.
   - Read Deuteronomy 30:19. What is the blessing?
     - ❖ The blessing is life: the restored Garden of Eden (kingdom of God) where God's people live in God's presence to experience the fullness of His blessing (great beauty, harmony, and peace). The tree of life in the garden of Eden symbolized the blessing of God in His presence.

4. What would be the result if the people did not fully obey all the law of God? *
   - If Israel did not fully obey all the law, they would be unrighteous and fall under the curse.
   - Read Deuteronomy 11:28. How does unrighteousness bring shame?
     - ❖ Like Adam, Israel's unrighteousness would make them guilty and would bring shame on them. If they broke the covenant, their honor would not be restored, but they would continue in the shame of Adam's sin that had corrupted the image of God in them, damaging their honor and diminishing their glory.
   - Read Deuteronomy 30:19. What is the curse?
     - ❖ The curse is death. In Genesis 3, God placed the curse of death on all of creation because of Adam's guilt. The curse of death is banishment to Sheol: The place of God's judgment after the death of the physical body where the souls of sinners are separated from His blessing to experience His anger and be punished under His curse with fire.

5. Is it possible for a person to fully obey all the law of God (follow all these laws all the time)? *
   *Note: If learners try to say they are generally good, remind them that the command is to do all the law, not merely most of the law, from the heart. Refer them to Genesis 8:21 in the Learner Guide. If they still try to say that they have obeyed all ten commands or that it is possible, let them

know that we will talk more about this later. Jesus provides a convincing answer in Matthew 5.
- Because we are born sinful from the heart and enemies of God, these laws are impossible to obey without failing in some way.

Wrap-up (10–15 minutes)

- Ask learners: What is the purpose of the lesson?
  - To understand the law of God and what happens if mankind obeys or disobeys His commands
- Ask learners: What is one new thing that you learned today?
- State to learners: Think about this **Key Lesson Question:**
  - What do you think will happen to you if you do not fully obey all the law of God?

LESSON 7
Promise of the Son-King

Review

1. What law did God give Adam? What laws did God give Israel?
2. How do the Ten Commandments show that mankind are sinners from the heart?
3. How much obedience to the law is required for a person to be righteous?
4. What is the punishment for disobeying the law of God? What was the result of Adam's sin?
5. What do you think will happen to you if you do not fully obey all the law of God?
6. What do we know about the promised Offspring of the woman?

Introduction

Purpose: To understand how the Son-King fulfills God's promises to restore every people group to His kingdom

Lesson 7 Context: After Moses died, Joshua led Israel into the promised land. For a couple hundred years, the Israelites were led by various prophets and warriors who sometimes followed God and sometimes disobeyed God. Then, the people of Israel rejected God as their king and asked God for a king like the nations around them. Their first king, Saul, rejected God and followed his own wicked way (1 Samuel 15).

Samuel Context: Samuel is a history of the transition from the times of the judges to the end of the reign of David. Samuel focuses on the life and reign of King David.

Vocabulary

- Anoint: To set someone apart for a holy purpose (ex. a king)
- Consecrate: To be set apart as holy for service to God (Mangum, Brown, Klippenstein, and Hurst 2014)
- Establish: To appoint a royal line of kings that will continue forever

- Revelation: The act of God making something known that was hidden

- Son-King: The greater King, the Son of David and Son of God, who will establish the kingdom of God on earth (Wellum 2021, 60)

- Trustworthy: "Able to be relied on to do or provide what is needed or right" (Merriam-Webster 2022)

Part I: A New King (1 Samuel 16:1–13)

The LORD said to Samuel, "How long will you mourn for Saul, since I have rejected him as king over Israel? Fill your horn with oil and be on your way; I am sending you to Jesse of Bethlehem. I have chosen one of his sons to be king." ² But Samuel said, "How can I go? If Saul hears about it, he will kill me." The LORD said, "Take a heifer with you and say, 'I have come to sacrifice to the LORD.' ³ Invite Jesse to the sacrifice, and I will show you what to do. You are to anoint for me the one I indicate." ⁴ Samuel did what the LORD said.

When he arrived at Bethlehem, the elders of the town trembled when they met him. They asked, "Do you come in peace?" ⁵ Samuel replied, "Yes, in peace; I have come to sacrifice to the LORD. Consecrate yourselves and come to the sacrifice with me." Then he consecrated Jesse and his sons and invited them to the sacrifice. ⁶ When they arrived, Samuel saw Eliab and thought, "Surely the LORD's anointed stands here before the LORD." ⁷ But the LORD said to Samuel, "Do not consider his appearance or his height, for I have rejected him. The LORD does not look at the things people look at. People look at the outward appearance, but the LORD looks at the heart." ⁸ Then Jesse called Abinadab and had him pass in front of Samuel. But Samuel said, "The LORD has not chosen this one either." ⁹ Jesse then had Shammah pass by, but Samuel said, "Nor has the LORD chosen this one." ¹⁰ Jesse had seven of his sons pass before Samuel, but Samuel said to him, "The LORD has not chosen these." ¹¹ So he asked Jesse, "Are these all the sons you have?"

"There is still the youngest," Jesse answered. "He is tending the sheep." Samuel said, "Send for him; we will not sit down until he arrives." ¹² So he sent for him and had him brought in. He was glowing with health and had a fine appearance and handsome features. Then the LORD said, "Rise and anoint him; this is the one." ¹³ So Samuel took the horn of oil and anointed him in the presence of his brothers, and from that day on the Spirit of the LORD came powerfully upon David.

Discussion

1. What happened to King Saul?
2. Read verse 3. What did God command the prophet Samuel to do?

3. Read verse 7. How does God see people differently than we do?
   - **Digging Deeper:** How did the Lord, who sees our hearts, describe the human heart?

"Every inclination of the human heart is evil from childhood." (Genesis 8:21)

4. Which son of Jesse did God choose? How is this surprising?
5. What did David experience after being anointed by Samuel?

Context: When David grew up, he replaced Saul as king and united the twelve tribes of Israel under his reign. During his reign, the prophet Nathan would give messages from God to David.

Part II: The Greater King (2 Samuel 7:4, 8–19, 28)

But that night the word of the Lord came to Nathan, saying…⁸ "Now then, tell my servant David, 'This is what the Lord Almighty says…⁹ I have been with you wherever you have gone, and I have cut off all your enemies from before you. Now I will make your name great, like the names of the greatest men on earth. ¹⁰ And I will provide a place for my people Israel and will plant them so that they can have a home of their own and no longer be disturbed. Wicked people will not oppress them anymore, as they did at the beginning ¹¹… I will also give you rest from all your enemies.'"

"The Lord declares to you that the Lord himself will establish a house for you: ¹² When your days are over and you rest with your ancestors, I will raise up your offspring to succeed you, your own flesh and blood, and I will establish his kingdom. ¹³ He is the one who will build a house for my Name, and I will establish the throne of his kingdom forever. ¹⁴ I will be his father, and he will be my son. When he does wrong, I will punish him with a rod wielded by men, with floggings inflicted by human hands …¹⁶ Your house and your kingdom will endure forever before me; your throne will be established forever." ¹⁷ Nathan reported to David all the words of this entire revelation.

¹⁸ Then King David went in and sat before the Lord, and he said: "Who am I, Sovereign Lord, and what is my family, that you have brought me this far? ¹⁹ You have spoken also of your servant's house for a great while to come, and this is instruction for mankind, O Lord God! …²⁸ Sovereign Lord, you are God! Your covenant is trustworthy, and you have promised these good things to your servant."

Discussion

1. How is David related to Abraham?
2. Read verse 8. What did God call David? What does a servant do?

3. Read verse 9. What are some things that God has already done for David?
4. How did the name Almighty encourage David? What is God promising David?
   - **Digging Deeper:** How does the promised kingdom fulfill the Garden of Eden?

Breakout Pivot: Kingdom through Covenant Chart

5. How will the covenant Offspring be related to David? How will the covenant Offspring be related to God?

2 Samuel 7:12: When your days are over and you rest with your ancestors, I will raise up your offspring to succeed you, *your own flesh and blood*, and I will establish his kingdom.	**2 Samuel 7:14:** I will be his *father*, and he will be my *son*.

6. Read verse 13. What does it mean that the Lord will build a house for His name?
   - **Digging Deeper:** How is the promised kingdom to David greater than the garden kingdom of Eden?

Genesis 2:8: Now the Lord God had *planted* a garden in the east, in Eden; and there he put the *man* he had formed.	**2 Samuel 7:10:** And I will provide a *place* for my people Israel and will *plant* them so that they can have a home of their own and no longer be disturbed.
Exodus 15:17-18: You will bring them [covenant people] in and plant them on the mountain of your inheritance—the place, Lord, you made for your dwelling, the sanctuary, Lord, your hands established. "The Lord reigns for ever and ever."	

7. How are the promises to David important for mankind?
   - **Digging Deeper:** The Son of Man refers to the Son of David as the last Adam who will restore the image of God in His people. Adam was the first son of man who ruled as God's representative on earth. Adam rebelled against God's rule, corrupting the image of God in mankind. God appointed Abraham and David as new rulers, like Adam, whose Offspring will restore the corrupted image of God in His people. The Son of Man is the greater Son-King who represents the covenant people to God and establishes the rule of God over the earth.

"What is man that you are mindful of him, and the *son of man* that you care for him? Yet you have made him a little lower than the heavenly beings and crowned him with glory and honor. You have given him dominion over the works of your hands." (Psalm 8:4–6 ESV)

Key Lesson Question: How is this promised Son-King different from other human kings?

Reminder: Scan this QR code to do the Meditation for this lesson and the Introduction for the next lesson:

Leader Guide

Objective: To describe some aspects of the promised kingdom, articulate key similarities between the Abrahamic and Davidic covenants, and trace the promise of Genesis 3:15 to the restoration of all nations to the kingdom of God through the greater Son-King, the Son of David and Son of God

Response: Because of God's promise through Adam, Abraham, and David, the greater Son-King will restore every people group to the kingdom of God.

Lesson Materials QR Code:

Review Activity (5 minutes): Refer to Lesson Materials.

Review (15–20 minutes)

1. What law did God give Adam? What laws did God give Israel?
   - God gave Adam the law not to eat of the tree of the knowledge of good and evil.
   - God gave Israel the Ten Commandments.

2. How do the Ten Commandments show that mankind are sinners from the heart?
   - Our sin against God begins in the heart. Our sinful thoughts and desires lead to sinful actions.

3. How much obedience to the law is required for a person to be righteous?
   - One hundred percent obedience to the law from the heart is required for a person to be counted righteous.

4. What is the punishment for disobeying the law of God? What was the result of Adam's sin?
   - The punishment for disobeying the law is death.
   - Mankind died under the curse of God being banished from the kingdom of God. Mankind became more and more evil. As the

righteous Lord over His creation, God delivered judgment by pouring out His anger on His enemies and allowing them to suffer for their sin because they had wronged their Lord and Creator.

5. What do you think will happen to you if you do not fully obey all the law of God?
   - I will remain under the curse of death. I will die and be sent to Sheol: The place of God's judgment after the death of the physical body where the souls of sinners are separated from His blessing to experience His anger and be punished under His curse with fire.

6. What do we know about the promised Offspring of the woman? (Genesis 3:15; 12:1-3)
   - The covenant Offspring will be a male descendant from the line of the offspring of promise through Abraham, Isaac, and Jacob who will defeat the power of death and restore all people groups to the kingdom of God.

Introduction (10 minutes): Refer to the lesson.

Lesson 7 (40–45 minutes)

Part I: A New King (1 Samuel 16:1–13)

1. What happened to King Saul? (v. 1)
   - God rejected Saul and was going to take away his kingdom.

2. Read verse 3. What did God command the prophet Samuel to do?
   - God commanded Samuel to go to the family of Jessie and anoint one of his sons to be the next king of Israel.

3. Read verse 7. How does God see people differently than we do? *
   - We look at the outside of people, their appearance, their family lineage, their wealth, their health, etc. God looks at the heart. God knows what people are thinking and who they really are.
   - **Digging Deeper:** How did the Lord, who sees our hearts, describe the human heart?
   *Note: Read Genesis 8:21 in the lesson.
     ❖ The heart of people is sinful from birth. God sees all our sin from its beginning to its end. Sin is not merely what we do but also what we think, desire, and feel.

4. Which son of Jesse did God choose? How is this surprising?
   - God chose David. David was not initially brought to Samuel but was left in the fields, watching sheep. It is surprising that the youngest brother who was a shepherd was chosen to be the next king. Normally, the oldest was preferred. In addition, a shepherd was not given much honor because tending sheep was considered a humble job.

5. What did David experience after being anointed by Samuel? (v. 13)
   - David was anointed to be the next king of Israel and received the power of the Holy Spirit.

Part II: The Greater King (2 Samuel 7:4, 8–19, 28)

1. How is David related to Abraham?
   *Note: Refer to the **Covenant Family Tree.**
   - David is a male descendant of Abraham.

2. Read verse 8. What did God call David? What does a servant do? *
   - God called David, "my servant." A servant follows the orders of his master.
   - Next lesson we will dig deeper into our understanding of a servant!

3. Read verse 9. What are some things that God has already done for David?
   - God has made David king; His presence has been with David, and He has cut off his enemies.
     - ❖ Cut off: To destroy completely and violently

4. How did the name Almighty encourage David? What is God promising David? *
   *Note: Point out the promises from the modal verb "will." Go through every verb with "will" and give the explanation. This will help them with future questions in this lesson.
   - Because God is the Lord Almighty, He has the power to fulfill His covenant promises.
     - ❖ Almighty: The only true God who possesses unlimited power over all things in heaven and on earth
   - I will make your name great: well known, honored, and prosperous.
   - I will provide a place for my people, Israel: a physical location on earth.
   - I will plant them so that they can have a home of their own: a safe place different from the nations around them.

- They will no longer be disturbed…I will also give you rest: a peaceful place.
- Wicked people will not oppress them: a place people are free from slavery and the influence of sin; a place of righteousness.
- Your house and your kingdom will endure forever before me: a place that will last forever, a divine kingdom, like the Garden of Eden.
- **Digging Deeper:** How does the promised kingdom fulfill the Garden of Eden?
  - ❖ The promised kingdom is the restored (greater) Garden of Eden where God's people live in God's presence to experience the fullness of His blessing (great beauty, harmony, and peace). It is the place where God's people dwell with God in righteousness, peace, and safety.

Breakout Pivot: Kingdom through Covenant Chart (15 minutes)

- **Fill in the blank directions** (5 minutes): Have them fill in the chart by writing the correct letter in the blank spaces using the word bank. Bring them back together as one group to clarify the right answers.
- **Compare and contrast directions** (5–10 minutes): Have them use the chart below to discuss the questions. Bring them back together as one group to clarify the right answers.
  - ❖ How are the promises to David similar to the ones God promised Abraham?
    - Both are promised a great name; both are promised a great kingdom (great size and great lineage); and both are promised an Offspring who will bless all peoples.
  - ❖ How did God promise to restore all nations to the kingdom through Abraham and David?
    - God promised to restore all nations to the kingdom through the covenant Offspring who would bless all people groups.

5. How will the covenant Offspring be related to David? How will the covenant Offspring be related to God? *

   *Note: Refer learners to the **Covenant Family Tree**. Then, explain:
   - The covenant Offspring will be fully human, the Son of David: 2 Samuel 7:12.
   - The covenant Offspring will be fully God, the Son of God: 2 Samuel 7:14.
   - **Summary:** The covenant Offspring is the Son-King who is both fully human and fully God because He is the Son of David and the Son of God.

6. Read verse 13. What does it mean that the Lord will build a house for His name?
   - The Lord will establish His eternal kingdom through the covenant Offspring, the greater Son-King, who is from the line of David and is the Son of God.
   - **Digging Deeper:** How is the promised kingdom to David greater than the garden kingdom of Eden?
     *Note: Read the verse table in the lesson.
     ❖ The kingdom that God promised to David through David's Offspring will be the new, greater Eden. Just as God planted Eden and set Adam over Eden as ruler, so the greater Son-King will restore God's rule, plant (strongly put) them in the greater Eden, the place of God's presence, and bring perfect peace.

7. How are the promises to David important for mankind? (vv. 16, 19) *
   - The promises are for mankind because the Son of David will restore all people groups to the kingdom of God as promised to Abraham and Adam and Eve. God will plant a greater Eden!
   - **Digging Deeper:** Refer to the lesson.

Wrap-up (10–15 minutes)

- Ask learners: What is the purpose of the lesson?
  ➢ To understand how the Son-King fulfills God's promises to restore every people group to His kingdom
- Ask learners: What is one new thing that you learned today?
- State to learners: Think about this **Key Lesson Question:**
  ➢ How is this promised Son-King different from other human kings?

LESSON 8
Prophecy of the Servant-King

Review

1. How is the promised Son-King different from other human kings?
2. What will the Son-King do?

Introduction

Purpose: To understand who the Servant-King is and how He brings victory over death

Context: Isaiah was a prophet to Judah who lived in the eighth century (740–700 BC). He prophesied right before Assyria conquered Judah as a judgment from God. Isaiah warned Judah about the consequences of disobeying God and the coming judgment. Isaiah also gave many prophecies of the coming restoration of the kingdom of God.

Vocabulary

- Afflict: To cause terrible mental or bodily pain
- Bear: To take and carry something that is difficult to hold, physically or mentally
- Despise: To strongly dislike or hate
- Disfigure/mar: To spoil or damage so that someone or something no longer looks beautiful
- Exalt: To raise to a higher rank or a more powerful position
- Heal: The act of God restoring the broken relationship (making peace) between God and sinners
- Justice: God's faithfulness to Himself to uphold the law by cursing (requiring full punishment) those who break the law and blessing (giving full reward) those who keep the law
- Justify: The act of God declaring a sinner righteous/not guilty according to the law of God
- Make intercession: The act of the Servant-King representing sinners to God through His greater sacrifice and His exaltation as the Son-King

- Pierce: To put a hole into something or someone
- Pour out: To empty oneself out physically so that a person no longer can continue living
- Satisfy: The act of God receiving the full payment that sinners deserve

Part I: Description of the Servant (Isaiah 52:13–14, 53:1–3)

See, my servant will act wisely; he will be raised and lifted up and highly exalted. ¹⁴ Just as there were many who were appalled at him—his appearance was so disfigured beyond that of any human being and his form marred beyond human likeness…

¹ Who has believed our message and to whom has the arm of the Lord been revealed? ²…He had no beauty or majesty to attract us to him, nothing in his appearance that we should desire him. ³ He was despised and rejected by mankind, a man of suffering, and familiar with pain. Like one from whom people hide their faces, he was despised, and we held him in low esteem.

Discussion

1. Read Isaiah 52:13. How is the Servant described?

2. Read 52:14–53:3. How does the description of the Servant change?
   - What does He look like?
   - How is He treated?
   - **Think about it:** The first description is in the future tense, "will be exalted," and the second description is in the past tense, "was afflicted."

Part II: Suffering of the Servant (Isaiah 53:4–9)

Surely, he took up our pain and bore our suffering, yet we considered him punished by God, stricken by him, and afflicted. ⁵ But he was pierced for our transgressions, he was crushed for our iniquities; the punishment that brought us peace was on him, and by his wounds we are healed. ⁶ We all, like sheep, have gone astray, each of us has turned to our own way; and the Lord has laid on him the iniquity of us all. ⁷ He was oppressed and afflicted, yet he did not open his mouth; he was led like a lamb to the slaughter, and as a sheep before its shearers is silent, so he did not open his mouth. ⁸…For he was cut off from the land of the living; for the transgression of my people he was punished. ⁹ He was assigned a grave with the wicked, and with the rich in his death, though he had done no violence, nor was any deceit in his mouth.

Discussion

1. Compare the people with the Servant:
    - Read verse 6. How are people described?
    - Read verse 7. What animal is the Servant compared to?
    - What is the difference between how the people and the Servant are described?

Part III: Accomplishment of the Servant (Isaiah 53:10–12)

Yet it was the LORD's will to crush him and cause him to suffer, and though the LORD makes his life an offering for sin, he will see his offspring and prolong his days, and the will of the LORD will prosper in his hand. [11] After he has suffered, he will see the light of life and be satisfied; by his knowledge my righteous servant will justify many, and he will bear their iniquities. [12] Therefore I will give him a portion among the great, and he will divide the spoils with the strong, because he poured out his life unto death, and was numbered with the transgressors. For he bore the sin of many, and made intercession for the transgressors.

Discussion

1. Read verse 10. Whose plan is it to crush the Servant? Why?

2. Look at verses 5 and 10–11. What will the Servant accomplish through his sacrifice?

Breakout Pivot: Sacrifice Chart

---

3. Compare Isaiah 53:8–9 and Isaiah 52:13; 53:11–12: What will happen to the Servant first? What will happen to the Servant second?

First, He dies…	Second, He will be raised to life…
For he *was cut off* from the land of the living; for the transgression of my people he was punished. He *was assigned a grave* with the wicked, and with the rich in his death, though he had done *no violence, nor was any deceit* in his mouth.	*After* he has suffered, he *will see the light of life*…I will give him a portion among the great, and he will divide the spoils with the strong, because he poured out his life unto death…he *will be raised* and lifted up and highly exalted.

4. Read verse 12. Who is the Servant? How does the Servant accomplish the restoration of the kingdom?
   - What are spoils?
   - Remember the promise about the Offspring of the woman (Genesis 3:15). What enemy does the Servant-King fight against? How will He win the fight?
   - Remember the blessing to Abraham. What are the "spoils" that the Servant-King will win?
5. Look at verse 12. What will the Servant-King do for the people?
6. How is the Servant-King the greater Son of Man (Adam, Abraham, and David)?

| **2 Samuel 7:12-13:** I will raise up your offspring to succeed you, your *own flesh and blood,* and I will establish his kingdom. He is the one who will build a house for my Name, and I will establish the throne of his kingdom forever. | **2 Samuel 7:14:** I will be his *father*, and he will be my *son*. |

Key Lesson Question: How can you be restored to right relationship with God in the kingdom of God?

Reminder: Scan this QR code to do the Meditation for this lesson and the Introduction for the next lesson:

Leader Guide

Objective: To describe the Servant, trace the progression from the First Sacrifice of Genesis 3:21 to the Final Sacrifice of the Servant-King as the greater Sacrifice, and articulate the Servant as the greater Son-King who will defeat death according to the prophecy of Genesis 3:15

Response: We can be restored to the kingdom of God through the Servant's sacrifice by believing in the greater Servant-King.

Lesson Materials QR Code:

Review Activity (10 minutes): Refer to Lesson Materials.

Review

1. How is the promised Son-King different from other human kings?
    - The promised Son-King is different because His rule is eternal over an eternal kingdom. Unlike other human kings, He will not have an end to His reign. The reason He will reign forever is that He is both the Son of God and the flesh and blood son of David. The Son-King will be both fully God and fully human.

2. What will the Son-King do?
    - He will restore all nations to the kingdom of God as promised to Abraham and Adam and Eve. This promise is for mankind. God will plant a greater Eden where God dwells with His people and rules from His throne (restored kingdom)!

Introduction (10 minutes): Refer to the lesson.

Lesson 8 (40–45 minutes)

Part I: Description of the Servant (Isaiah 52:13–14, 53:1–3)

1. Read Isaiah 52:13. How is the Servant described?
   - The servant is described as wise and exalted.

2. Read 52:14–53:3. How does the description of the Servant change? *
   - The Servant is now described as experiencing great shame and suffering.
   - What does He look like? (52:14; 53:2–3)
     - ❖ His appearance is described as disfigured, marred, without beauty or majesty, not desirable.
   - How is He treated?
     - ❖ He is despised, rejected by mankind, and knows suffering and pain.
   - **Think about it:** The first description is in the future tense, "will be exalted," and the second description is in the past tense, "was afflicted."
     - ❖ First, the Servant was afflicted (past tense) with great shame. The past tense means that the suffering and shame will happen before He is raised and exalted.
     - ❖ Second, the Servant will be raised, lifted, and highly exalted (future tense) to a position of great honor. The future tense means that He will be raised and exalted after He experiences suffering and shame.

Part II: Suffering of the Servant (Isaiah 53:4–9)

1. Compare the people with the Servant:
   - Read verse 6. How are people described? What kind of sheep are they?
     - ❖ People are described as sheep who have gone astray and are full of iniquity (sin).
   - Read verse 7. What animal is the Servant compared to? What kind of sheep is He?
     - ❖ The Servant is compared to a sheep led to the slaughter—a righteous (without deceit), sacrificed sheep.
   - What is the difference between how the people and the Servant are described?
     - ❖ People are *rebellious* sheep that have *disobeyed* the Father (v. 6), while the Servant is a *righteous* sheep without *deceit* (v. 9) who is *slaughtered* as the *sacrifice* for sin (v. 7).

Part III: Accomplishment of the Servant (Isaiah 53:10–12)

1. Read verse 10. Whose plan is it to crush the Servant? Why? *
    - It is the plan of God (Lord's will) to sacrifice the Servant to make His life an offering/sacrifice for sin and guilt.
    - **Think about it:** Because God is just, there must be a blood payment for sin to remove guilt and cover shame. Because we cannot obey the law perfectly, we deserve the punishment of sin: death. There are only two ways the sin debt can be paid: either people die taking their own punishment for sin or the Servant takes the punishment they deserve through His death as the greater Sacrifice.

2. Look at verses 5 and 10–11. What will the Servant accomplish through his sacrifice? *
    - God will heal sinners from the wounds of sin by taking their guilt and pain on Himself. He will heal the relationship between Himself and sinners by restoring sinners to relationship with God through His greater sacrifice. Healing brings peace with God.
    - God will *pour out* His righteous anger on the Servant to *satisfy* God's justice.
        - ❖ Justice: God's faithfulness to Himself to uphold the law by cursing (requiring full punishment) those who break the law and blessing (giving full reward) those who keep the law
    - The Servant will bring peace between God and sinners by taking the anger of God against His enemies and by justifying them.
      *Note: Ask questions to fill out the **Relational Account Diagram.** Then, explain:
        - ❖ The Servant will *justify* sinners by taking their sin debt and crediting them with righteousness so that their relationship with God is restored. Sinners are blessed not by their own obedience to the law but by the Servant who credits them with righteousness through faith alone.
        - ❖ Isaiah uses the word servant/slave to describe how He will take human shame on Himself by bearing the guilt of sin as the greater Sacrifice for sin. Because He will be fully human, He will experience the shame of human existence, yet without sin, and pay the sin debt in full for humans as the Servant/Slave of God.

Breakout Pivot: Sacrifice Chart (10–15 minutes)

- **Fill in the blank directions** (5 minutes): Separate learners into groups of two or three. Have them fill in the chart by writing the correct letter in the blank spaces using the word bank. Bring them back together as one group to clarify the right answers.
    - ❖ Learner 1: What is the first story about the sacrifice of an animal that removes guilt through the spilled blood and covers shame?
    - ❖ Learner 2: The first story about the sacrifice of an animal that removes guilt through the spilled blood and covers shame is the First Sacrifice (**C**).
- **Compare and contrast directions** (5 minutes): Send them back into groups. Have them use the chart below to discuss the questions. Bring them back together as one group to clarify the right answers.
    - ❖ How is the sacrifice of the Servant different?
        - The Servant is not an animal but is human.
    - ❖ How is the Servant's death connected to the sacrifices we have talked about before?
        - The sacrifices of the animals symbolized the coming Servant's death. The sacrifices described how the Servant will restore every people group to relationship with God and to the kingdom of God through His substitutionary death as the greater Sacrifice.
        - Example: From the first sacrifice, we learn that the Servant-King will remove guilt through His spilled blood and cover shame.

3. Compare Isaiah 53:8–9 and Isaiah 52:13; 53:11–12: What will happen to the Servant first? What will happen to the Servant second?
    - First, the Servant was afflicted (*past tense*) with great shame in His death. Second, He will be exalted (*future tense*) with great honor in His resurrection. The Servant "will see the light of life." He will be raised (52:13) back to life.

4. Read verse 12. Who is the Servant? How does the Servant accomplish the restoration of the kingdom? *
    - The Servant is the exalted Son-King who will restore the nations to the kingdom of God.
    - What are spoils?
        - ❖ Spoils: The valuable possessions gained by those who have won a war
        - ❖ Often a king will return home with spoils when he is victorious in war.

- Remember the promise about the Offspring of the woman (Genesis 3:15). What enemy does the Servant-King fight against? How will He win the fight?
  - ❖ He fights against the snake/Satan.
  - ❖ He will win by crushing the head of the snake–He will defeat sin and death by dying to pay the sin debt and by rising again in victory over death.
- Remember the blessing to Abraham. What are the "spoils" that the Servant-King will win?
  - ❖ The spoils are the nations for whom He takes the sin debt, credits with righteousness, and restores to the kingdom of God (Genesis 12:1-3).

5. Look at verse 12. What will the Servant-King do for the people?
   - The Servant-King will make intercession for His people so that they don't receive the punishment they deserve.
     - ❖ Intercession: The act of the Servant-King representing sinners to God through His greater sacrifice and His exaltation as the Son-King

6. How is the Servant-King the greater Son of Man (Adam, Abraham, and David)? *Note: Read the verse table in the lesson and refer to the **Covenant Family Tree**. Then explain:
   - The Servant-King will represent the covenant people to God and will establish the rule of God over the earth as the exalted Son-King, the Son of David and the Son of God.

Wrap-up (10–15 minutes)
*Note: If the learners decide not to continue, use the Gospel Invitation in Appendix I to explain the gospel and to call them to Jesus for salvation.
- Ask learners: What is the purpose of the lesson?
  - ➢ To understand who the Servant-King is and how He brings victory over death
- Ask learners: What is one new thing that you learned today?
- State to learners: Think about this **Key Lesson Question**:
  - ➢ How can you be restored to right relationship with God in the kingdom of God?

LESSON 9
Revelation of the King

Review

1. Why is there a coming Servant?
2. Who is He and what will happen to him?
3. How would He change the relationship between God and mankind?

Introduction

Purpose: To identify the family history of Jesus and recognize who He is and what He will do

Lesson Context: Matthew was one of Jesus's close followers, called the twelve disciples. Matthew focuses on Jesus's three-year ministry and describes Jesus as the promised Son-King who saves His people from sin and establishes the kingdom of God.

Vocabulary

- Christ ("anointed one")/Messiah: The promised Offspring of the woman (greater King) who was anointed to defeat sin and death
- Conceive: The moment a woman becomes pregnant
- Consummate: To have sex for the first time with your spouse after your wedding
- Disgrace: To bring shame on someone
- Expose: To make something known to the public
- Fulfill: To complete what was promised in the covenants
- Immanuel: God with us
- Most High: The name of God that shows Him as the highest rank above everything else; the most important
- Overshadow: The covenantal act of the Holy Spirit covering someone with the presence of God to create new life
- Pledge: To make a promise to a person/group that cannot be broken

- Reign: The period of time that a king or queen rules over a place
- Son of Man: The promised Servant-King (Isaiah 53) and Son-King (2 Samuel 7) who represents the covenant people to His Father and establishes the rule of God over the earth
- Virgin: Someone who has never had sex

Part I: Mary Is Found With Child (Matthew 1:1, 18–25)

The book of the genealogy of Jesus Christ, the son of David, the son of Abraham…[18] This is how the birth of Jesus the Messiah came about: His mother Mary was pledged to be married to Joseph, but before they came together, she was found to be pregnant through the Holy Spirit. [19] Because Joseph her husband was faithful to the law, and yet did not want to expose her to public disgrace, he had in mind to divorce her quietly. [20] But after he had considered this, an angel of the Lord appeared to him in a dream and said, "Joseph son of David, do not be afraid to take Mary home as your wife, because what is conceived in her is from the Holy Spirit.[21] She will give birth to a son, and you are to give him the name Jesus, because he will save his people from their sins." [24] When Joseph woke up, he did what the angel of the Lord had commanded him and took Mary home as his wife. [25] But he did not consummate their marriage until she gave birth to a son. And he gave him the name Jesus.

Discussion

1. Read verse 1. From whom is Jesus descended?
   - **Digging Deeper:** What do we know about the promised Offspring of Abraham and David?

2. Read verse 18. What was the relationship between Mary and Joseph?

3. What's different about how this baby was conceived? Why was the baby born this way?
   - **Digging Deeper:** Remember how Isaiah described the Servant in Isaiah 53:9 as "without deceit." The Offspring of the woman must be perfect … just as the sacrificial offerings had to be perfect without blemish (perfect, male lamb).

Genesis 1:1-2: In the beginning God *created* the heavens and the earth. Now the earth was formless and empty, darkness was over the surface of the deep, and the Spirit of God was *hovering over* the waters.	**Luke 1:35:** The Holy Spirit will *come on you*, and the power of the Most High will *overshadow you*. So the holy one to be born will be called the Son of God.

4. Who is Joseph, how is he described, and what were his actions?

Luke Context: Luke was a physician who investigated the events of Jesus's life and wrote down an accurate history of Jesus's life from eyewitnesses. Luke gives us the fullest and longest description of Jesus's birth, including the early events from before Jesus's birth to a brief description of Jesus's childhood. Luke focuses on Jesus as the Son of Man who saves His people and on the role of the Holy Spirit in Jesus's ministry.

Part II: The Birth of Jesus Announced (Luke 1:26–38)

In the sixth month of Elizabeth's pregnancy, God sent the angel Gabriel to Nazareth, a town in Galilee, ²⁷ to a virgin pledged to be married to a man named Joseph, a descendant of David. The virgin's name was Mary. ²⁸ The angel went to her and said, "Greetings, you who are highly favored! The Lord is with you." ²⁹ Mary was greatly troubled at his words and wondered what kind of greeting this might be. ³⁰ But the angel said to her, "Do not be afraid, Mary; you have found favor with God. ³¹ You will conceive and give birth to a son, and you are to call him Jesus. ³² He will be great and will be called the Son of the Most High. The Lord God will give him the throne of his father David, ³³ and he will reign over Jacob's descendants forever; his kingdom will never end." ³⁴ "How will this be," Mary asked the angel, "since I am a virgin?" ³⁵ The angel answered, "The Holy Spirit will come on you, and the power of the Most High will overshadow you. So the holy one to be born will be called the Son of God. ³⁶ Even Elizabeth your relative is going to have a child in her old age, and she who was said to be unable to conceive is in her sixth month. ³⁷ For nothing will be impossible with God"³⁸ "I am the Lord's servant," Mary answered. "May your word to me be fulfilled." Then the angel left her.

Discussion

1. Read verses 26–27. What did the angel say about the birth of Mary's child? How is this possible?
    - **Digging Deeper:** Isaiah prophesied about the birth of Jesus seven hundred years before it happened. Isaiah wrote, "Therefore the Lord himself will give you a sign: The virgin will conceive and give birth to a son, and will call him Immanuel." (Isaiah 7:14)

2. What did the angel say about Mary's child?
    - **Digging Deeper:** What have we previously learned about the Servant-King that is like Luke 1:32–34?

Luke 1:32-33, 35: He will be great and will be called the Son of the Most High. The Lord God will give him the throne of *his father David*, and he will reign over Jacob's descendants forever; his kingdom will never end...So the holy one to be born will be called the *Son of God*.	**2 Samuel 7:12-14:** I will raise up your offspring to succeed you, *your own flesh and blood*, and I will establish his kingdom. He is the one who will build a house for my Name, and I will establish the throne of his kingdom forever. "I will be *his father*, and he will be *my son*."

3. Read verse 38. How did Mary respond to the angel's words?

Part III: The Birth of Jesus (Luke 2:1-7 & Matthew 1:22-23)

In those days Caesar Augustus issued a decree that a census should be taken of the entire Roman world...³ And everyone went to their own town to register. ⁴ So Joseph also went up from the town of Nazareth in Galilee to Judea, to Bethlehem the town of David, because he belonged to the house and line of David. ⁵ He went there to register with Mary, who was pledged to be married to him and was expecting a child. ⁶ While they were there, the time came for the baby to be born, ⁷ and she gave birth to her firstborn, a son. She wrapped him in clothes and placed him in a manger, because there was no guest room available for them.

Matthew 1:22–23

All this took place to fulfill what the Lord had said through the prophet: ²³ "The virgin will conceive and give birth to a son, and they will call him Immanuel" (which means "God with us").

Discussion

1. Why did Joseph and Mary go to Bethlehem? Why is this significant?
    - **Digging Deeper:** Micah prophesied seven hundred years before Jesus's birth that the Messiah would be born in Bethlehem and would be the greater King: "But you, Bethlehem Ephrathah, though you are small among the clans of Judah, out of you will come for me one who will be ruler over Israel, whose origins are from of old, from ancient times." (Micah 5:2)

2. What kind of child would this be? Where was He born? How is this surprising?

Luke 1:32-33: He will be great and will be called the Son of the Most High. The Lord God will give him the throne of his father David, and he will reign over Jacob's descendants forever; his kingdom will never end.	**Luke 2:7:** She gave birth to her firstborn, a son. She wrapped him in clothes and placed him in a manger, because there was no guest room available for them.

- **Digging Deeper:** How does this connect with the appearance of the servant in Isaiah's prophecy?

"He had no beauty or majesty to attract us to him, nothing in his appearance that we should desire him." (Isaiah 53:2)

Breakout Pivot: Image of God Chart

3. What names are given to Jesus? What do they mean? What will Jesus do?

Key Lesson Question: Think about Jesus's birth and names. Who is Jesus and what will He do?

Reminder: Scan this QR code to do the Meditation for this lesson and the Introduction for the next lesson:

Leader Guide

Objective: To articulate who Jesus is and what He will do as the promised Offspring in connection with Adam and Eve, Abraham, and David; identify Jesus as both fully man and fully God from birth; and explain how Jesus's virgin birth is the fulfillment of the promises

Response: Because Jesus is the promised Offspring of Adam, Abraham, and David, He is the promised Son of Man.

Lesson Materials QR Code:

Review Activity (5 minutes): Refer to Lesson Materials.

1. In groups of two or three, discuss how the Servant-King provides salvation for sinners. Use the **Sin and Sacrifice Mind Map** as a guide.
   - The Servant-King provides salvation by crushing the head of the snake by offering Himself as the greater Sacrifice in the place of sinners. The Servant-King takes the guilt of sinners by paying their sin debt and covers their shame by crediting them with righteousness.

Review (5–10 minutes)

1. Why is there a coming Servant?
   - God will sacrifice the Servant, His Son, as the covenant sacrifice that takes the curse of the covenant and restores the relationship between God and His covenant people.

2. Who is He and what will happen to him?
   - In this sacrifice, the promised Son-King, Son of David and Son of God, will pay the sin debt for sinners by taking the punishment of sin on Himself and crediting them with righteousness.
   - Then He will rise again (resurrect) as the exalted Son-King over the eternal kingdom of God.

3. How would He change the relationship between God and mankind?
   - All those who put their faith in the greater Sacrifice will be saved from judgment and credited with righteousness.

Introduction (10 minutes): Refer to the lesson.

Background Material

At the end of the Old Testament, we encounter sadness that mankind continues to withdraw from God and that His people who He has loved so much continue to reject Him and break the covenant. They longed for the Servant-King and Savior who will restore the relationship between God and His people. (The original readers would have felt their own coming destruction and longed for the hope of the coming Savior.)

After Isaiah, God continued to send more prophets with various messages about judgment for sin and hope in the coming Servant-King. Because the people refused to listen to God, He often allowed other nations to conquer the Israelites. The Assyrians and Babylonians conquered them. Eventually, the Persians let the Israelites rebuild. As time passed, the Greeks and Romans invaded. In the New Testament, we will see the Israelites living under Roman rule, hoping for the Servant-King to restore the people of God to the kingdom of God.

Fun Facts

- There are around four hundred years between the Old Testament and the New Testament.
- Testament also can be translated as covenant.
- Gospel: The good news of who Jesus is and what Jesus did for sinners
- The Gospels: The four Gospels are the written description of Jesus's life from four different eyewitness accounts.

Lesson 9 (40–45 minutes)

Part I: Mary Is Found with Child (Matthew 1:1, 18–25)

1. Read verse 1. From whom is Jesus descended? *
   - Refer to the **Covenant Family Tree** to show that Jesus is descended from Abraham and David.

- **Digging Deeper:** What do we know about the promised Offspring of Abraham and David?
  - ❖ The promised Offspring is ...
    - a descendant of Abraham, Isaac, Israel, and David
    - the Offspring of Abraham who would bless all nations by restoring all nations to the kingdom of God through the covenant by the substitutionary sacrifice
    - the Son of Man:
      - ➢ The *Servant-King* who will crush the head of the snake by being crushed by God as the sacrifice for sin to restore the relationship between God and all nations
      - ➢ The greater *Son-King* who represents the covenant people to His Father and establishes the rule of God over the earth

2. Read verse 18. What was the relationship between Mary and Joseph?
   - They were engaged to be married.

3. What's different about how this baby was conceived? Why was the baby born this way? (v. 18) *
   *Note: Read the verse table in the lesson. Avoid getting into a prolonged discussion now on the Trinity as this is one of the biggest mysteries of the Bible and is difficult to understand. Briefly use the **Trinity Chart** to describe the Trinity. Then, continue with the lesson.
   - This baby was conceived through the creative power of the Holy Spirit. Joseph did not contribute anything to the birth of Jesus.
     - ❖ The Holy Spirit is God. The act of overshadowing is an act of creation that can only be true of God. As the Spirit participated in the first creation in Genesis 1, so the Spirit participated in the creation of the human nature of Jesus. Jesus had a real human birth through the virgin Mary. He is truly the Offspring of the woman.
     - ❖ Jesus is the Son of Man, who has always existed as the Son of God, and in His human birth *added* to Himself a human nature through the creative work of the Spirit (Wellum 2021, 79).
   - Every human being who is a descendent from Adam is born a sinner and will die (Psalm 51:5). However, because this baby was not born from a human father, He did not inherit the sinful nature of Adam. The Holy Spirit protected Jesus's human nature from being corrupted by sin.
   - **Digging Deeper:** Refer to the lesson.

4. Who is Joseph, how is he described, and what were his actions? (vv. 18–20)
   - Joseph is a descendant of David. Because Mary is married to Joseph, she becomes part of Joseph's family line. Though Jesus is not the physical son of Joseph, He is in the family line of Joseph.
   - He is described as faithful to the law. He wanted to put her away because of possible adultery (Ten Commandments).
     - ❖ He did not want "to expose her to public disgrace (shame)."
     - ❖ He believed the word of the angel and obeyed (vv. 24–25).

Luke Context: Refer to the lesson.

Part II: The Birth of Jesus Announced (Luke 1:26–38)

1. Read verses 26–27. What did the angel say about the *birth* of Mary's child? How is this possible?
   - The child would be born of a virgin woman by the power of the Holy Spirit. With man, this is impossible, but with God all things are possible.
   - That Mary is a virgin means that Mary did nothing shameful and was not guilty of breaking the law.
   - **Digging Deeper:** Refer to the lesson.

2. What did the angel say about Mary's *child*? (vv. 32–34) *
   - He will be great (the Son of the Most High), sit on the throne of David, reign over Jacob's descendants, and establish the kingdom forever.
     - ❖ Most High: The name of God that shows Him as the highest rank above everything else; the most important
   - **Digging Deeper:** What have we previously learned about the Servant-King that is like Luke 1:32–34?

   *Note: Read the verse table in the lesson to review and compare.
     - ❖ The Servant-King is the greater Son-King who represents the covenant people to God and establishes the rule of God over the earth.

3. Read verse 38. How did Mary respond to the angel's words?
   - Mary called herself the servant of the Lord and responded with humble faith.

Part III: The Birth of Jesus (Luke 2:1–7; Matthew 1:22–23)

1. Why did Joseph and Mary go to Bethlehem? Why is this significant? (vv. 1–5) *
   - Mary and Joseph went to Bethlehem to be registered for a census. It is significant because it reveals that Joseph was a descendant of David.
   - **Digging Deeper:** Refer to the lesson.

2. What kind of child would this be? Where was He born? How is this surprising? *

   *Note: Read the verse table in the lesson.
   - He will be the Son-King, the Son of David and Son of God: Luke 1:32–33.
   - He was born in a manger, a place where animals eat: Luke 2:7.
   - **Summary:** Though announced as a king, the Messiah was laid in a manger. This was a description of someone who was poor. It was a humble birth, like that of the poorest of the land.
   - **Digging Deeper:** How does it connect with the appearance of the servant in Isaiah's prophecy?
     - ❖ Isaiah describes him as having no beauty or majesty. This means he would not have the appearance and honor people might expect a king to have.

Breakout Pivot: Image of God Chart (5–10 minutes)

- **Fill in the blank directions:** Separate learners into groups of two or three. Have them fill in the chart by writing the correct word in the blank spaces using the word bank. Bring them back together as one group to clarify the right answers.
  - ❖ Learner 1: How will the Son of Man restore the image of God in man?
  - ❖ Learner 2: He will restore the image of God in man with glory and honor.

3. What names are given to Jesus? What do they mean? What will Jesus do? *
   *Note: In the New Testament (written in Greek), there is no distinction between the two meanings of Lord and Lord. Lord means both Lord and Lord. Thus, the Lord is the personal name of God that shows Him as the sovereign King over all nations.
   - Names of Jesus: Son of David, Son of Abraham, Savior (meaning of His name), Christ/Messiah, Son of the Most High, Holy One, and Immanuel.
   - Jesus is the promised Offspring of Adam, Abraham, and David:
     *Note: After collecting the names of Jesus, write down Christ/Messiah and Son of Man on a whiteboard and write out the descriptions below.
     - ❖ Christ ("anointed one")/Messiah: The promised Offspring of the woman (greater King) who was anointed to defeat sin and death
     - ❖ Son of Man: The promised Servant-King (Savior) and Son-King (Immanuel: Son of the Most High and Son of David) who represents the covenant people to His Father and establishes the rule of God over the earth
   - **Summary:** Jesus, the Messiah and Son of Man, has come to defeat sin and death, to save His people from their sins, and to restore all nations to the kingdom of God.

Wrap-up (10–15 minutes)

- Ask learners: What is the purpose of the lesson?
  - ➢ To identify the family history of Jesus and recognize who He is and what He will do
- Ask learners: What is one new thing that you learned today?
- State to learners: Think about this **Key Lesson Question:**
  - ➢ Think about Jesus's birth and names. Who is Jesus and what will He do?

LESSON 10
Kingdom Law Fulfilled

Review

1. What was different about how Jesus was conceived? Why was Jesus born this way?

2. Think about Jesus's birth and names. Who is Jesus and what will He do?

Introduction

Purpose: To recognize Jesus as fully God and fully man and describe how He obeys the law fully for us

Vocabulary

- Abolish: To put an end to a law or a rule that has been put in place

- Disciples: Jesus's closest followers whom He taught and prepared to continue His work

- Sheol/Hell: The place of God's judgment after the death of the physical body where the souls of sinners are separated from His blessing to experience His anger and be punished under His curse with fire

- Lustfully: Having intense sexual want for someone who is not your husband or wife

- Persecute: To cause someone mental or physical hurt because of their beliefs

Part I: Jesus's Teaching on the Law (Matthew 5:1–2, 17–18)

Now when Jesus saw the crowds, he went up on a mountainside and sat down. His disciples came to him, ² and he began to teach them…¹⁷ "Do not think that I have come to abolish the Law or the Prophets; I have not come to abolish them but to fulfill them. ¹⁸ For truly I tell you, until heaven and earth disappear, not the smallest letter, not the least stroke of a pen, will by any means disappear from the Law until everything is accomplished."

Discussion

1. What is the law of God? How much obedience to the law is required for a person to be righteous?
2. What did Jesus come to do?
3. How much of the law will Jesus obey?
4. Why is it necessary for Jesus to be fully human to satisfy the requirements of the law?

Part II: The Heart of the Law (Matthew 5:21–22, 27–28, 43–45, 48)

"You have heard that it was said to the people long ago, 'You shall not murder, and anyone who murders will be subject to judgment.' ²² But I tell you that anyone who is angry with a brother or sister will be subject to judgment…And anyone who says, 'You fool!' will be in danger of the fire of hell."

²⁷ "You have heard that it was said, 'You shall not commit adultery.' ²⁸ But I tell you that anyone who looks at a woman lustfully has already committed adultery with her in his heart."

⁴³ "You have heard that it was said, 'Love your neighbor and hate your enemy.' ⁴⁴ But I tell you, love your enemies and pray for those who persecute you, ⁴⁵ that you may be children of your Father in heaven. He causes his sun to rise on the evil and the good, and sends rain on the righteous and the unrighteous. ⁴⁸ Be perfect, therefore, as your heavenly Father is perfect."

Discussion

1. Is disobedience only something that we do or say outwardly, or is it also something we desire and think on the inside? Why?
    - **Digging Deeper:** Remember the explanation of the Ten Commandments. Jesus's teaching is a good explanation of the law because the law does not only require that you do right actions but also that you "love the Lord your God with all your heart and with all your soul and with all your strength" (Deuteronomy 6:5) and that you "love your neighbor as yourself" (Leviticus 19:18). Because our thoughts and desires are not always loving, our desires are as sinful as our actions.

"Every inclination of the human heart is evil from childhood." (Genesis 8:21)

"Love...God with All Your Heart." (Deuteronomy 6:4-5)	Sin of the Heart towards God
1. You shall have no other gods.	
2. You shall not make an image or bow down to an image of anything in heaven or on earth.	
3. You shall not misuse the name of the LORD.	
4. Remember the Sabbath day by keeping it holy.	
"Love Your Neighbor as Yourself." (Leviticus 19:18)	**Sin of the Heart towards Man**
5. Honor your father and your mother.	
6. You shall not murder.	
7. You shall not commit adultery.	
8. You shall not steal.	
9. You shall not bear false testimony against your neighbor.	
10. You shall not covet.	

2. What is the punishment for sin? Think about the story of Adam and Eve and of Noah.

3. According to verse 48, what does God require of us?
   - Can we do what God commands? Why or why not?

4. Why is it necessary for us that Jesus be fully human and fully God?
   - **Digging Deeper:** What does the title Son of Man tell us about Jesus?

Breakout Pivot: Relational Account Diagram

Key Lesson Question: If one person hates someone and another person murders someone, are they both equally guilty before God? Why?

Reminder: Scan this QR code to do the Meditation for this lesson and the Introduction for the next lesson:

Leader Guide

Objective: To recognize Jesus as fully God and fully man, articulate why it was necessary for Jesus to fulfill the law and the prophets fully, and describe our inability to obey the law fully and how that affects our relationship with God

Response: Because we cannot fully obey the law, Jesus, the Son of Man, obeyed the law fully for us.

Lesson Materials QR Code:

Review Activity (5–10 minutes): Refer to Lesson Materials.

1. How did Abraham have a sin debt?
    - Abram was a sinner, like everyone who comes from Adam, and came from a family that worshiped idols.

2. How did Abraham receive righteousness?
    - Abram received righteousness through faith alone in the Lord. Abram, like all mankind, was born with an account full of sin as an enemy of God. We call it the sin debt. When Abram put his faith in the Lord, God replaced his sin debt with a credit of righteousness. Because of this righteousness that was given by the Lord, Abram was forgiven and accepted by God. Abram went from being an enemy of God to being restored to relationship with God as his Lord through faith alone.

3. Did Abraham deserve righteousness? Why or why not?
    - No, he did not. First, God initiated the relationship with Abram through the covenant. Second, The works of mankind only contribute to a greater sin debt. When someone works at a job, he deserves the reward for his work. However, Abram did not work for his righteousness. Instead, God walked through the pieces of the sacrifice by Himself symbolizing that He will do what the covenant requires and take the curse of the broken covenant. Because God will do the work for Abram, Abram doesn't deserve it. The covenant relationship

is a gift from God that can only be received through faith in the Lord. The covenant is by grace alone through faith alone.

Review (10–15 minutes)

1. What was different about how Jesus was conceived? Why was Jesus born this way?
    - Jesus was conceived through the Holy Spirit who overshadowed the virgin Mary. Joseph did not contribute to the birth of Jesus.
        - ❖ The Holy Spirit is God. The act of overshadowing is an act of creation that can only be true of God. As the Spirit participated in the first creation in Genesis 1, so the Spirit participated in the creation of the human nature of Jesus. Jesus had a real human birth through the virgin Mary. He is truly the Offspring of the woman.
        - ❖ Jesus is the Son of Man, who had always existed as the Son of God, and in His human birth *added* to Himself a human nature through the creative work of the Spirit (Wellum 2021, 79).
    - Every human being who is a descendent from Adam is born a sinner and will die (Psalm 51:5). However, because Jesus was not born from a human father, He did not inherit the sinful nature of Adam. The Holy Spirit protected Jesus's human nature from being corrupted by sin.

2. Think about Jesus's birth and names. Who is Jesus and what will He do?
    - He is the promised Offspring of Adam, Abraham, and David:
        - ❖ Messiah: The promised Offspring of the woman (greater King) who was anointed to defeat sin and death
        - ❖ Son of Man: The promised Servant-King (Savior) and Son-King (Immanuel: Son of the Most High and Son of David) who represents the covenant people to His Father and establishes the rule of God over the earth
    - Jesus, the Messiah and Son of Man, has come to defeat sin and death, to save His people from their sins, and to restore all nations to the kingdom of God.

Introduction (5–10 minutes): Refer to the lesson.

Lesson 10 (40–45 minutes)

Part I: Jesus's Teaching on the Law (Matthew 5:1–2, 17–18)

1. What is the law of God? How much obedience to the law is required for a person to be righteous?
   - The law of God is summarized in the Ten Commandments.
   - One hundred percent obedience to the law from the heart is required for a person to be counted righteous.

2. What did Jesus come to do? (vv. 17–18)
   - Jesus came to fulfill (to complete what was promised in the covenants) the law fully, every part to the very last word and the smallest part of a word.

3. How much of the law will Jesus obey? (v. 18) *
   *Note: The learner may not understand why Jesus is righteous at this point. The goal is for them to be thinking about why Jesus is fulfilling the law and earning a *human righteousness*. Identify Jesus as fully human and fully God.
   - Jesus obeys all the law. He is completely righteous.

4. Why is it necessary for Jesus to be fully human to satisfy the requirements of the law?
   - The law requires full obedience from a human because humans have broken the law. The righteousness Jesus has as the Son of God cannot be given to a human. The Son of God added to Himself a human nature so He could earn a perfect human righteousness that can be given to humans.

Part II: The Heart of the Law (Matthew 5:21–22, 27–28, 43–45, 48)

1. Is disobedience only something that we do or say outwardly or is it also something we desire and think on the inside? Why?
   - Disobedience to the law involves the mind, desires, and emotions. Our actions are a result of what we think and desire because we do what we think is best and desire most. Because we do what we think is best and desire most to do, our thoughts and desires are as sinful as our actions.
   - **Digging Deeper:** Refer to the lesson.
     *Note: As a group, fill in the second column of the **Ten Commandments Chart** to show how sin comes from the heart. The goal is to show the connection of sinful desire and thought to sinful action.

2. What is the punishment for sin? Think about the story of Adam and Eve and of Noah. (v. 22)
   - The punishment for sin is death in Hell/Sheol, the place of God's judgment after the death of the physical body where the souls of sinners are separated from His blessing to experience His anger and be punished under His curse with fire.

3. According to verse 48, what does God require of us? *
   - God requires perfection, which is full obedience to His law.
   - Can we do what God commands? Why or why not?
     ❖ We cannot do what God commands because we do not always love God with all our being, and we do not always love our neighbor as ourselves. We have broken God's law in our thoughts, desires, and feelings. We are enemies of God.

4. Why is it necessary for us that Jesus be fully human and fully God? *
   - Because the first son of man, Adam, broke the law, the requirements of the law can only be satisfied by another human, the greater Son of Man. Since the law requires perfection and only God can be perfect, Only Jesus who is both fully God and fully man can obey the law fully and earn a perfect human righteousness.
   - **Digging Deeper:** What does the title Son of Man tell us about Jesus?
     ❖ The Son of Man is the title for the promised Servant-King (Isaiah 53) and Son-King (2 Samuel 7) who represents the covenant people to His Father and establishes the rule of God over the earth.

Breakout Pivot: Relational Account Diagram (10 minutes)

- **Directions:** Separate learners into groups of two or three. Have them use the **Relational Account Diagram** to discuss the questions. Bring them back together as one group to clarify the right answers.
    - ❖ Why do we have a sin debt?
        - We earned our sin debt by disobeying the law of God. Our works contribute to our sin debt.
    - ❖ What is the sin debt?
        - The sin debt is death. We earn death because the punishment of sin is death.
    - ❖ What is the credit?
        - The obedience of Jesus is the credit of righteousness. Jesus earned a perfect human righteousness according to the law of God.
    - ❖ How are sinners credited righteousness?
        - Sinners are credited righteousness through faith alone in the greater Sacrifice. Jesus, the greater Sacrifice, will pay the sin debt and replace the sin debt with His human righteousness.

Wrap-up (10–15 minutes)

- Ask learners: What is the purpose of the lesson?
    - ➢ To recognize Jesus as fully God and fully man and describe how He obeys the law fully for us
- Ask learners: What is one new thing that you learned today?
- State to learners: Think about this **Key Lesson Question:**
    - ➢ If one person hates someone and another person murders someone, are they both equally guilty before God? Why?

LESSON 11
Sacrifice of the King

Review

1. If one person hates someone and another person murders someone, are they both equally guilty before God? Why or why not?

2. How much of the law did Jesus obey? Why did Jesus need to earn human righteousness?

3. Abraham said, "God himself will provide the lamb for the burnt offering."
   - In the Garden of Eden, why did God kill the animal and clothe Adam and Eve?
   - What did God provide as a sacrifice instead of Isaac?
   - It was said, "On the mountain of the LORD it will be provided." (Genesis 22:14) What did this mean?

4. In Isaiah 53, who is the Servant and what will happen to Him?

Introduction

Purpose: To understand the mercy of God toward sinners through Jesus, the greater Sacrifice

Vocabulary

- Criminal: Someone who has broken the law
- Deserve: To earn something because of one's work
- Forgiveness: The act of God releasing sinners from a sin debt
- Forsake: The act of God turning away His love from and pouring out His righteous anger on His Son
- Gave up His spirit: To allow (Himself) to die
- Good news/gospel
  ❖ The message of the kingdom of God about the greater Sacrifice of the Messiah
  ❖ The truth of who Jesus is and what He did to save sinners through His birth, life, death, resurrection, and ascension

5. Mercy: The act of God not punishing a sinner who deserves punishment because He has extended forgiveness

6. Repentance/Repent: The act of turning away from your sin and turning to the LORD as your God and King

Part I: Forgiven at the Cross (Luke 23:26, 33–43)

As the soldiers led him away, they seized Simon from Cyrene, who was on his way in from the country, and put the cross on him and made him carry it behind Jesus …³³ When they came to the place called the Skull, they crucified him there, along with the criminals—one on his right, the other on his left. ³⁴ Jesus said, "Father, forgive them, for they do not know what they are doing." And they divided up his clothes by casting lots. ³⁵ The people stood watching, and the rulers even sneered at him. They said, "He saved others; let him save himself if he is God's Messiah, the Chosen One." ³⁶ The soldiers also came up and mocked him. They offered him wine vinegar ³⁷ and said, "If you are the king of the Jews, save yourself." ³⁸ There was a written notice above him, which read: this is the king of the Jews.

³⁹ One of the criminals who hung there hurled insults at him: "Aren't you the Messiah? Save yourself and us!" ⁴⁰ But the other criminal rebuked him. "Don't you fear God," he said, "since you are under the same sentence? ⁴¹ We are punished justly, for we are getting what our deeds deserve. But this man has done nothing wrong." ⁴² Then he said, "Jesus, remember me when you come into your kingdom." ⁴³ Jesus answered him, "Truly I tell you, today you will be with me in paradise."

Discussion

1. What was the name of the place where the soldiers led Jesus?
   - **Digging Deeper:** This is the place where Jesus, the Offspring of the woman, would crush the head (skull) of Satan, the snake.

2. How did Jesus experience shame?
   - **Digging Deeper:** How does this fulfill the prophecy of Isaiah?

"He was despised and rejected by mankind, a man of suffering, and familiar with pain. Like one from whom people hide their faces he was despised, and we held him in low esteem." (Isaiah 53:3)

3. Read verse 34. What did Jesus say about the people who were crucifying Him? What do we learn about Jesus from these words on the cross?

4. What were the people watching the crucifixion saying about Jesus? Was it true?

5. With whom was Jesus crucified? What was different about one of the criminals?

6. What did Jesus say to the criminal who believed in Him?
   - **Digging Deeper:** Paradise is the restored Garden of Eden (kingdom of God) where God's people live in God's presence to experience the fullness of His blessing (great beauty, harmony, and peace).

"The LORD will surely comfort Zion and will look with compassion on all her ruins; he will make her deserts like Eden, her wastelands like the garden of the LORD. Joy and gladness will be found in her, thanksgiving and the sound of singing." (Isaiah 51:3)

7. How was God's forgiveness of the criminal an act of mercy? How does God justly forgive sinners?
   - **Digging Deeper:** What did Noah, Abraham, David, and this criminal have in common? How did God show mercy to Noah, Abraham, David, and this criminal?

Noah-Salvation: *Not deserved* Genesis 4:20-21	Then Noah built an altar to the LORD…he *sacrificed burnt offerings* on it. The LORD smelled the pleasing aroma and said in his heart: "Never again will I curse the ground because of humans, even though *every inclination of the human heart is evil from childhood.*
Abraham-Covenant: *Not deserved* Genesis 15:6	Abram *believed* the LORD, and he *credited* it to him as righteousness.
David-Kingdom: *Not deserved* 2 Samuel 7:18-19, 28	*Who am I,* Sovereign LORD, and what is my family, that you have brought me this far?…Your covenant is trustworthy, and you have promised these good things to your servant.
Criminal-Forgiveness: *Not deserved* Luke 23:41-43	"We are punished justly, for we are getting what our deeds *deserve.* But this man has done nothing wrong." Then he said, "Jesus, remember me when you come into your kingdom." Jesus answered him, "Truly I tell you, today you will be with me in paradise."

Part II: Forsaken at the Cross (Matthew 27:45–46, 51, 54)

From noon until three in the afternoon darkness came over all the land. ⁴⁶ About three in the afternoon Jesus cried out in a loud voice, "Eli, Eli, lema sabachthani?" (which means "My God, my God, why have you forsaken me?") …⁵¹ At that moment the curtain of the temple was torn in two from top to bottom. The earth shook, the rocks split …⁵⁴ When the centurion and those with him who were guarding Jesus saw the earthquake and all that had happened, they were terrified, and exclaimed, "Surely he was the Son of God!"

John 19:28–30

Later, knowing that everything had now been finished, and so that scripture would be fulfilled, Jesus said, "I am thirsty." ²⁹ A jar of wine vinegar was there, so they soaked a sponge in it, put the sponge on a stalk of the hyssop plant, and lifted it to Jesus's lips. ³⁰ When he had received the drink, Jesus said, "It is finished." With that, he bowed his head and gave up his spirit.

Discussion

1. What did Jesus cry out on the cross? Why did God forsake His Son on the cross?

Breakout Pivot: Sacrifice Chart

2. What did the Roman soldier say about Jesus? Why?
   - **Digging Deeper:** When God poured out His anger in the flood, He destroyed the earth by shaking the earth violently. Throughout the Bible, God shakes the nations because of His anger toward His enemies. The anger of God is His response to sin that is consistent with the purity of His character and comes out of His righteous rule over His creation. As the righteous Lord over His creation, God delivers judgment by pouring out His anger on His Son because His Son bears the sins of many on Himself.

3. What does it mean that Jesus "gave up his Spirit"?
   - **Digging Deeper:** How did Jesus fulfill the words "On the mountain of the Lord it will be provided"?

4. How does Jesus fulfill (finish) the promise about the Offspring of the woman and the snake through the prophecy of the Servant-King (Isaiah 52:13–53)?

Promise of the Offspring	Prophecy of the Servant-King
Genesis 3:21: The LORD God made garments of skin for Adam and his wife and clothed them. **Genesis 3:15:** And I will put enmity between you and the woman, and between your offspring and hers; he will *crush* your head, and you will strike his heel	**Isaiah 53:10-11:** Yet it was the LORD's will to *crush* him and cause him to suffer, and though the LORD makes his life an offering for sin, he will see his offspring and prolong his days, and the will of the LORD will prosper in his hand. After he has suffered, he will see the light of life and be satisfied; by his knowledge my righteous servant will justify many, and he will bear their iniquities.

Key Lesson Question: In what sense are we all criminals? How is salvation possible for even the worst criminal?

Reminder: Scan this QR code to do the Meditation for this lesson and the Introduction for the next lesson:

THE BIG STORY

Leader Guide

Objective: To explain the significance of Jesus's words on the cross in fulfillment of Old Testament prophecy, understand the necessity for faith in the sacrifice, and recognize Jesus as the Son of Man from Genesis 3:15

Response: Because Jesus paid the sin debt, we should believe in Him to set us free from our sins by exchanging His righteousness for our sin debt.

Lesson Materials QR Code:

Review Activity (5 minutes): Refer to Lesson Materials.

Review (10–15 minutes)

1. If one person hates someone and another person murders someone, are they both equally guilty before God? Why or why not?
    - Both are equally guilty because the desire and the action are both sinful. Our actions are a result of what we think and desire. We do what we think is best and desire most. Because we do what we think is best and desire most to do, our thoughts and desires are as sinful as our actions.

2. How much of the law did Jesus obey? Why did Jesus need to earn human righteousness?
    - Jesus obeyed the law fully. The law requires full obedience from a human because a human broke the law. Jesus did not need righteousness for Himself because He is the perfect Son of God. The Son of God came to earth and took on a full humanity in the person of Jesus to earn human righteousness according to the law for us so He could credit us His human righteousness.

3. Abraham said, "God himself will provide the lamb for the burnt offering."
      - In the Garden of Eden, why did God kill the animal and clothe Adam and Eve?
        - ❖ Because of their sin, they deserved death. God killed the animal and clothed Adam and Eve to cover their shame with the skins of the animal and to remove their guilt through its spilled blood.
      - What did God provide as a sacrifice instead of Isaac?
        - ❖ God provided a ram as a sacrifice instead of his son.
      - It was said, "On the mountain of the Lord it will be provided" (Genesis 22:14). What did this mean?
        - ❖ The grammar is in the future tense, meaning the animal sacrifice is a symbol that points to the greater Sacrifice who will come later. This verse hints that there is a coming Sacrifice that will restore sinners' relationship to God. Through the greater Sacrifice, God will provide the debt payment for sin and remove guilt from His people.

   4. In Isaiah 53, who is the Servant and what will happen to Him?
      - In this sacrifice, the promised Son of David and Son of God will pay the sin debt for His people by taking the punishment of sin on Himself and crediting them with His human righteousness. Then He will rise again (resurrect) as the exalted Son-King over the eternal kingdom of God.

Introduction (5–10 minutes): Refer to the lesson.

Lesson 11 (40–45 minutes)

Part I: Forgiven at the Cross (Luke 23:26, 33–43)

1. What was the name of the place where the soldiers led Jesus? (v. 33)
   - "the skull"
   - **Digging Deeper:** Refer to the lesson.

2. How did Jesus experience shame?
   - Jesus was mocked, ridiculed, insulted, and hung naked on a cross with two criminals. Crucifixion is one of the most shameful deaths that has been invented by mankind.
   - **Digging Deeper:** How does this fulfill the prophecy of Isaiah? *Note: Read Isaiah 53:3 in the lesson.
     - ❖ Jesus was rejected by everyone: His closest followers, the Jewish people, and the Roman authorities. Jesus was made fun of,

THE BIG STORY

whipped many times, had a crown of thorns pressed onto His head, and was made to suffer terribly. Jesus was placed on a cross to die, hanging naked for all to see.

3. Read verse 34. What did Jesus say about the people who were crucifying Him? What do we learn about Jesus from these words on the cross?
   - "Father, forgive them, for they do not know what they are doing."
   - This reveals that the mercy of God through Jesus was offered to all, even to those who were in the act of murdering Him. Jesus was speaking out of His humanity. He was expressing His desire for God's mercy for sinners.

4. What were the people watching the crucifixion saying about Jesus? Was it true? (v. 35)
   - The people were mocking Him saying, "He saved others; let him save himself if he is God's Messiah, the Chosen One." They were correct that Jesus is the Messiah, even though they didn't believe the truth.
   - They were saying true statements with wrong intentions. Although they didn't believe it, their statement was still true.

5. With whom was Jesus crucified? What was different about one of the criminals? (vv. 37–41)
   - Two criminals: One of the criminals repented of his sin and believed in Jesus and defended Jesus; the other mocked Him.
     - ❖ Repent: The act of turning away from your sin and turning to the LORD as your God and King

6. What did Jesus say to the criminal who believed in Him? (v. 43) *
   *Note: Read Isaiah 51:3 in the lesson.
   - Jesus said, "Truly I tell you, today you will be with me in paradise."
   - **Digging Deeper:** Refer to the lesson.

7. How was God's forgiveness of the criminal an act of mercy? How does God justly forgive sinners? *
   *Note: Use the **Relational Account Diagram** as a visual.
   - For God to forgive sin, someone must pay the sin debt. Jesus paid the criminal's sin debt so that the relationship between God and the criminal was restored.
   - God's mercy does not mean that He overlooks sin or allows sin to be unpunished. Because all mankind is born sinful from the heart, they are enemies of God who is just and merciful. Because God requires

the sin debt to be paid, He sent Jesus, His Son, to pay the sin debt for sinners. Sinners who repent of their sin and believe in Jesus to save them from their sin receive mercy because Jesus took the punishment they deserve. Through Jesus, the enemies of God are restored to relationship with God.
- **Digging Deeper:** What do Noah, Abraham, David, and this criminal have in common? How did God show mercy to Noah, Abraham, David, and this criminal?
  - ❖ Noah, Abraham, David, and the criminal are sinners who deserve to be punished for their sins. They do not deserve righteousness from God.
  - ❖ He is showing mercy to them because He gives them what they have not earned and what they do not deserve. The criminal had no chance to do anything to earn God's favor. He had no obedience to show God. He was forgiven because of what Jesus did, not what He had done. Like Noah, Abraham, and David, the criminal only had faith in Jesus as the Lamb of God to pay His sin debt and credit Him with His human righteousness so He could be restored to the kingdom of God.

Part II: Forsaken at the Cross (Matthew 27:45–46, 51, 54; John 19:28–30)

1. What did Jesus cry out on the cross? Why did God forsake His Son on the cross? (v. 46)
   - "My God, my God, why have you forsaken me?"
   - God forsook Jesus because Jesus was bearing the guilt of the people on His body. Because God is holy, He cannot look on sin. In that moment, the Father turned His love away from His Son and poured out His anger on His Son.

Breakout Pivot: Sacrifice Chart (10–15 minutes)

- **Directions:** Separate learners into groups of two or three. Have them use the **Sacrifice Chart** to discuss the questions. Bring them back together as one group to clarify the right answers.
  - ❖ How does Jesus, the Servant-King, fulfill the covenant sacrifice (restoration)?
    - Jesus, the Son of God, takes the covenant curse on Himself and dies as the Sacrifice for His people to restore them to right relationship with God.

- ❖ How does Jesus, the Servant-King, fulfill the burnt offering (substitution)?
  - Jesus removes sinners' guilt through His spilled blood by dying in their place to restore them to right relationship with God.
- ❖ How does Jesus, the Servant-King, fulfill the first sacrifice (victory over sin and death) and the final sacrifice (justification)?
  - The power of sin and death is the law because we are under the judgment of the law. Until the law is satisfied, there can be no forgiveness. Only when Christ satisfied the law through His life and death could we be free from the power of sin and death.
  - This is the victory of the cross: Jesus bears His people's guilt on Himself and covers their shame and credits them with His righteousness. By satisfying the requirements of the law, Jesus, fully man, freed sinners from the judgment of the law. Death and sin no longer have any authority, and Satan's power through sin and death has been crushed. Jesus, fully God, has taken the curse of the covenant and given His people life. The true King has waged war against the enemy and won a decisive victory.

---

2. What did the Roman soldier say about Jesus? Why? (v. 54)
   - "Surely he was the Son of God!" (v. 54). He saw what was happening to the earth and sky, how "darkness came over all the land" (v. 45), and "the earth shook, the rocks split" (v. 51). He heard the words of Jesus and saw His mercy. The evidence confirmed that Jesus is the Son of God.
   - **Digging Deeper:** Refer to the lesson.

3. What does it mean that Jesus "gave up his Spirit?"
   - It means that Jesus allowed Himself to die. Nobody forced Jesus to die. Jesus willingly allowed His enemies to take Him and kill Him. Jesus died.
   - **Digging Deeper:** How did Jesus fulfill the words "On the mountain of the LORD it will be provided?"
   *Note: Refer to the **Sin and Sacrifice Mind Map** as a visual aid.
     - ❖ Jerusalem is in the same mountain range as Moriah, where Abraham was to sacrifice Isaac. Jesus is the greater Sacrifice who would come later. This verse points to Jesus as the greater Sacrifice who restores sinners' relationship to God. Jesus is the substitutionary sacrifice that God promised to provide as the debt payment for sin that removes guilt from His people.

4. How does Jesus fulfill (finish) the promise about the Offspring of the woman and the snake through the prophecy of the Servant-King (Isaiah 52:13–53)? (v. 30)
   - Jesus, the Offspring of the woman, crushes the head of the snake by being crushed for sinners. Jesus pays the sin debt by receiving the anger of God instead of sinners, removing their guilt through His blood, and covering their shame and credits them with His human righteousness so that they would be restored to life in relationship to the Father. They are restored to the kingdom of God to live under God's rule. Death has been crushed (defeated)!

Wrap-up (10–15 minutes)

- Ask learners: What is the purpose of the lesson?
  - ➤ To understand the mercy of God toward sinners through Jesus, the greater Sacrifice
- Ask learners: What is one new thing that you learned today?
- State to learners: Think about this **Key Lesson Question:**
  - ➤ In what sense are we all criminals? How is salvation possible for even the worst criminal?

LESSON 12
Exaltation of the King

Review

1. What was different about one of the criminals? What did Jesus say to him?
2. In what sense are we all criminals? How is salvation possible for even the worst criminal?
3. How does God justly forgive sinners?
4. How does Jesus fulfill (finish) the promise about the Offspring of the woman and the snake through the prophecy of the Servant-King (Isaiah 52:13–53)?

Introduction

Purpose: "That you may believe that Jesus is the Messiah, the Son of God, and that by believing you may have life in his name" (John 20:31)

Vocabulary

- Ascend (v)/Ascension (n):
  - ❖ Verb: To go upward
  - ❖ Noun: Jesus's exaltation to the Father to sit on the throne and rule over the kingdom of God as the chosen representative of the new humanity
- High day: The day of a religious festival
- Rise: To come back to life from death
- Tomb: A place for people to bury their dead

Part I: Proof of Jesus's Death (John 19:31–42)

Since it was the day of Preparation, and so that the bodies would not remain on the cross on the Sabbath (for that Sabbath was a high day), the Jews asked Pilate that their legs might be broken and that they might be taken away. ³² So the soldiers came and broke the legs of the first, and of the other who had been crucified with him. ³³ But when they came to Jesus and saw that he was already dead, they did not break his legs. ³⁴ But one of the soldiers pierced his side with a spear, and at once there came out blood and water. ³⁵ He who saw it has borne witness—his testimony is true, and he knows that he is telling the truth—that you also may believe....³⁸ Later, Joseph of Arimathea asked Pilate for the body of Jesus ...⁴¹ At the place where Jesus was crucified, there was a garden, and in the garden a new tomb, in which no one had ever been laid ... ⁴² They laid Jesus there ...

Discussion

1. How do we know that Jesus died? What proof is there?
2. Where was Jesus's body laid?
   - **Digging Deeper:** What is significant about the garden?

Genesis 2:8: Now the LORD God had planted a *garden* in the east, in Eden; and there he put the man he had formed.	**John 19:41-42:** At the place where Jesus was crucified, there was a garden, and in the *garden* a new *tomb*, in which no one had ever been laid...they laid Jesus there.

Part II: Burial and Resurrection of Jesus (John 20:1–18)

Early on the first day of the week, while it was still dark, Mary Magdalene went to the tomb and saw that the stone had been removed from the entrance. ² So she came running to Simon Peter and the other disciple, the one Jesus loved, and said, "They have taken the Lord out of the tomb, and we don't know where they have put him!" ³ So Peter and the other disciple started for the tomb. ⁴ Both were running, but the other disciple outran Peter and reached the tomb first. ⁵ He bent over and looked in at the strips of linen lying there but did not go in. ⁶ Then Simon Peter came along behind him and went straight into the tomb. He saw the strips of linen lying there, ⁷ as well as the cloth that had been wrapped around Jesus' head. The cloth was still lying in its place, separate from the linen. ⁸ Finally the other disciple, who had reached the tomb first, also went inside. He saw and believed. ⁹ (They still did not understand from Scripture that Jesus had to rise from the dead.) ¹⁰ Then the disciples went back to where they were staying.¹¹ Now Mary stood outside the tomb crying ...¹⁴ She turned around and saw Jesus standing there, but she did not realize that it was

Jesus. ¹⁵ He asked her, "Woman, why are you crying? Who is it you are looking for?" Thinking he was the gardener, she said, "Sir, if you have carried him away, tell me where you have put him, and I will get him." ¹⁶ Jesus said to her, "Mary." She turned toward him and cried out in Aramaic, "Rabboni!" (which means "Teacher"). ¹⁷ Jesus said, "Do not hold on to me, for I have not yet ascended to the Father. Go instead to my brothers and tell them, 'I am ascending to my Father and your Father, to my God and your God.'" ¹⁸ Mary Magdalene went to the disciples with the news: "I have seen the Lord!" And she told them that he had said these things to her.

Discussion

1. Which three people saw the empty tomb?
   - **Digging Deeper:** How does the empty tomb fulfill the promise of the Offspring of the woman and the snake?

> See, my servant will act wisely; he will be raised and lifted up and *highly exalted* …Yet it was the LORD's will to *crush* him and cause him to suffer …After he has suffered, he will see the light of life and be satisfied; by his knowledge my righteous servant will *justify* many, and he will bear their iniquities. Therefore I will give him a portion among the great, and he will divide the *spoils* with the strong, because he poured out his life unto death, and was numbered with the transgressors. For he bore the sin of many, and made intercession for the transgressors. (Isaiah 52:13, 53:10–12)

2. Who was the first person to see Jesus alive again? How do we see Jesus's love for her?

3. What did Jesus want her to tell the disciples?
   - **Digging Deeper:** Jesus, as the Son of Man, was going back to His Father to sit on the throne of the kingdom of God and to restore all nations to the kingdom through His birth, life, death, resurrection, and ascension. As fully man, Jesus effectively represents His people to the Father because only a perfect human can represent another human. As fully God, Jesus can intercede effectively to the Father because He uniquely has access to the Father as the Son. As a human, Jesus has a relationship with humans. As God, Jesus has a relationship with God. Because Jesus is united to both God and man, He alone can intercede effectively to God for man.

Part III: Jesus's Appearing to His Disciples (John 20:19–31)

On the evening of that first day of the week, when the disciples were together, with the doors locked for fear of the Jewish leaders, Jesus came and stood among them and said, "Peace be with you!" [20] After he said this, he showed them his hands and side. The disciples were overjoyed when they saw the Lord. [21] Again Jesus said, "Peace be with you! As the Father has sent me, I am sending you." [22] And with that he breathed on them and said, "Receive the Holy Spirit…" [24] Now Thomas (also known as Didymus), one of the Twelve, was not with the disciples when Jesus came. [25] So the other disciples told him, "We have seen the Lord!" But he said to them, "Unless I see the nail marks in his hands and put my finger where the nails were, and put my hand into his side, I will not believe." [26] A week later his disciples were in the house again, and Thomas was with them. Though the doors were locked, Jesus came and stood among them and said, "Peace be with you!" [27] Then he said to Thomas, "Put your finger here; see my hands. Reach out your hand and put it into my side. Stop doubting and believe." [28] Thomas said to him, "My Lord and my God!" [29] Then Jesus told him, "Because you have seen me, you have believed; blessed are those who have not seen and yet have believed." [30] Jesus performed many other signs in the presence of his disciples, which are not recorded in this book. [31] But these are written that you may believe that Jesus is the Messiah, the Son of God, and that by believing you may have life in his name.

Discussion

1. What did Jesus tell the disciples the first time He saw them? Why?
   - **Digging Deeper:** What did Jesus give to the disciples? How is breathing the Spirit into the disciples a symbol of new life?

   "Then the LORD God formed a man from the dust of the
   ground and breathed into his nostrils the breath of life,
   and the man became a living being." (Genesis 2:7)

2. Who was missing from the disciples? What did he think when he heard the news about Jesus?

3. What did Jesus show Thomas? How did Thomas respond?
   - What do you think about Thomas's response? How did Jesus show love to Thomas? Do you have the same response? If so, what is Jesus saying to you?

4. Who did Jesus say was blessed? Why was this book written?

Breakout Pivot: Kingdom through Covenant Chart

Key Lesson Question: Refer to Appendix I.

> "For 'Everyone who calls on the name of the Lord will be saved.'" (Romans 10:13)

Reminder: Scan this QR code to do the Meditation for this lesson:

Leader Guide

Objective: To recognize Jesus's death and resurrection as the fulfillment of Genesis 3:15, 21 and Isaiah 53, analyze Jesus's birth, life, death, resurrection, and ascension in light of who He is and what He did, and evaluate the call to repentance and faith in Jesus

Response: Because Jesus is the resurrected Son of Man, we should believe in Him as our personal Lord and Savior.

Lesson Materials QR Code:

Review Activity (5 minutes): Refer to Lesson Materials.

Review (10–15 minutes)

1. What was different about one of the criminals? What did Jesus say to him?
   - One of the criminals put his faith in Jesus. Jesus promised him entrance into the kingdom of God.

2. In what sense are we all criminals? How is salvation possible for even the worst criminal?
   - We are all criminals because we have all disobeyed the law of God and are under the judgment of the law. Because Jesus paid the sin debt by dying the death we deserved, we can be forgiven of our sin. Because Jesus lived a perfect life, we can be credited with His human righteousness. This salvation can be ours through faith alone in Jesus as our Lord God, substitute sacrifice, and King.

3. How does God justly forgive sinners?
   - God's mercy does not mean that He overlooks sin or allows sin to be unpunished. Because all mankind are born sinful from the heart, they are enemies of the just and merciful God. Because God requires the sin debt to be paid, He sent Jesus, His Son, to pay the sin debt for sinners who repent of their sin and believe in Jesus. Sinners receive mercy because Jesus took the punishment they deserve.

4. How does Jesus fulfill (finish) the promise about the Offspring of the woman and the snake through the prophecy of the Servant-King (Isaiah 52:13–53)?
   - Jesus, the Offspring of the woman, crushes the head of the snake by being crushed for sinners. Jesus takes the curse of death on Himself and pays the sin debt by bearing their guilt through His spilled blood, covering their shame, and crediting them with His human righteousness so that they would be restored to relationship to the Father and to the kingdom of God to live under God's rule. Death has been crushed (defeated)!

Introduction (5 minutes): Refer to the lesson.

Lesson 12 (40–45 minutes)

Part I: Proof of Jesus's Death (John 19:31–42)

1. How do we know that Jesus died? What proof is there? (vv. 33–34) *
   - The soldiers saw that Jesus was already dead. When they stabbed his side, water and blood came out. This only happens if a person is dead. The soldiers, His enemies who killed him, gave testimony to his death.

2. Where was Jesus's body laid? (v. 41) *
   - Jesus's body was laid in Joseph's tomb in a garden.
   - **Digging Deeper:** What is significant about the garden?
     *Note: Read the verse table in the lesson.
     - ❖ The Garden of Eden was the first place of God's kingdom. The promise of the Offspring of the woman crushing the head of the snake happened in the Garden of Eden. Jesus's garden burial after His sacrifice is a sign of the coming restoration of the kingdom in the greater Eden.

Part II: Burial and Resurrection of Jesus (John 20:1–18)

1. Which three people saw the empty tomb? (v. 9) *
   - Mary, Peter, and the other disciple saw the empty tomb.
   - **Digging Deeper:** How does the empty tomb fulfill the promise about the Offspring of the woman and the snake?
     *Note: Read Isaiah 52:13 and 53:10–12 in the lesson.
     - ❖ Jesus is the Offspring of the woman who went to war with the snake who holds power over mankind through sin and death. Jesus crushed the head of the snake by being crushed by the Father as the final sacrifice for sinners. Through His death as the Servant-King, He justified His people through His greater sacrifice. Through His resurrection as the exalted Son-King, He takes the spoils of His victory over Satan by restoring the nations to the kingdom of God.

2. Who was the first person to see Jesus alive again? How do we see Jesus's love for her?
   - Mary was the first to see Jesus when He came back to life. Jesus showed His love by appearing to Mary and revealing Himself to Mary. His voice sparked her memory.

3. What did Jesus want her to tell the disciples?
   *Note: For the Digging Deeper, refer to the passage from Isaiah 52–53 in question 1 of Part II.
   - He is going back to the Father.
   - **Digging Deeper:** Refer to the lesson.

Part III: Jesus's Appearing to His Disciples (John 20:19–31)

1. What did Jesus tell the disciples the first time He saw them? Why? (v. 19)
   - Jesus said, "Peace be with you." Jesus knew they were hiding from the Jewish leaders.
   - **Digging Deeper:** What did Jesus give to the disciples? How is breathing the Spirit into the disciples a symbol of new life?
     *Note: Read Genesis 2:7 in the lesson.
     - ❖ Jesus gave the disciples the Holy Spirit.
     - ❖ When the Lord God created man, He breathed into him life. Now, Jesus, the Lord God, breathes the Holy Spirit into them, giving them new life and filling them with the presence of God.

2. Who was missing from the disciples? What did he think when he heard the news about Jesus? (v. 24)
   - Thomas was missing. He would not believe unless he saw proof.

3. What did Jesus show Thomas? How did Thomas respond? (v. 27) *
   - Jesus showed Thomas the scars on His hands, feet, and side to prove His resurrection to Thomas. Thomas responds with a confession of faith that he believed Jesus to be his Lord and his God.
   - What do you think about Thomas's response? How did Jesus show love to Thomas? Do you have the same response? If so, what is Jesus saying to you?
     *Note: The last two parts are meant for the learners to reflect on but only share if they want to and feel comfortable.
     ❖ Learner's Response
     ❖ Jesus revealed Himself to Thomas and showed him proof, even though Thomas doubted. Jesus rebuked Thomas but still loved him and showed him His hands and side, even though He didn't have to.

4. Who did Jesus say was blessed? Why was this book written? (vv. 28–31) *
   - Jesus said that those who did not see but still believed were blessed.
   - Jesus said, "But these are written that you may believe that Jesus is the Messiah, the Son of God, and that by believing you may have life in his name."
   - Jesus is the promised male Offspring (fully human) who defeated death and the promised Son of God (fully God) who is restoring all nations to the kingdom of God. In the name of Jesus alone, we have life through the victory of Christ!

Breakout Pivot: Kingdom through Covenant Chart (10 minutes)

- **Directions:** Refer them to the **Kingdom through Covenant Chart** as a guide to help them remember what they have learned. Not all the answers are in the chart. Bring them back together as one group to clarify the right answers.
  ❖ How is Jesus the last Adam?
    ▪ Jesus is the Offspring of the woman who crushed the head of the snake by defeating sin and death and restores the nations to the greater Eden, the kingdom of God.
  ❖ How did Jesus restore the nations to the kingdom of God in His birth, life, death, resurrection and ascension?

- Jesus took on human nature in His sinless birth:
  - ➢ Jesus is the Son-King, who has always existed as the Son of God, and in His human birth *added* to Himself a human nature through the creative work of the Spirit (Wellum 2021, 60 and 79), forever joining the presence of God with man in His body as one person, fully God and fully man.
- Jesus fulfilled the condition of the new covenant in His life:
  - ➢ Jesus is the last Adam who fully obeyed God and earned a complete human righteousness.
- Jesus took the curse of the covenant in His substitutionary death.
  - ➢ Jesus is the greater Sacrifice (the guilt-bearing Sacrifice who pays the sin debt) who restores the nations to covenant relationship with God.
- Jesus established the kingdom in His resurrection and ascension:
  - ➢ Jesus is the Son of Man who restores the relationship between God and His covenant people and is going to His Father to represent the covenant people and establish the rule of God over the earth.

Wrap-up (15–20 minutes)

- Ask learners: What is the purpose of the lesson?
  - ➢ "That you may believe that Jesus is the Messiah, the Son of God, and that by believing you may have life in his name." (John 20:31)

- Ask learners: What is one new thing that you learned today?

- Discuss with Learners: Continue to Appendix I and go through the Good News Questions, Invitation, and Covenant Promise.

APPENDIX I
Gospel Invitation

Learner Guide

Gospel Reflection

1. Why is man's relationship to God broken?
2. As the Son-King, who is Jesus?
3. As the Servant-King, what did Jesus do to save sinners?

Gospel Questions

1. Why is your relationship to God broken?
2. As the Son-King, who do you believe Jesus is?
3. As the Servant-King, what do you believe Jesus did to save you?
4. Will you call on Jesus for salvation from your sin by repenting of your sin, believing in Jesus's life, death, and resurrection in your place, and submitting to Jesus as your Lord and God?

> If you declare with your mouth, "Jesus is Lord," and believe in your heart that God raised him from the dead, you will be saved. For it is with your heart that you believe and are justified, and it is with your mouth that you profess your faith and are saved ... Everyone who calls on the name of the Lord will be saved. (Romans 10:9–10, 13)

Covenant Promise

Therefore he [Jesus] is able to save completely those who come to God through him [Jesus], because he [Jesus] always lives to intercede for them. (Hebrews 7:25)

Leader Guide

State to Learners: Jesus is the Servant-King who died to pay our sin debt and rose again as the exalted Son-King.
*Note: Ask these questions to discern if they understand the gospel. If they understand the gospel, continue to the next set of questions ("Invite Learners").
1. Why is man's relationship to God broken?
    - All mankind are sinners who have broken God's law.

2. As the Son-King, who is Jesus?
    - Jesus is fully man and fully God.

3. As the Servant-King, what did Jesus do to save sinners?
    - Jesus died in the place of sinners to pay their sin debt, credited them with righteousness, and came back to life to represent His people to the Father.

Invite Learners: The Call of Jesus
*Note: Ask these questions to discern if they believe the gospel and will call on Christ to save them. If they repent and believe in the gospel, give them the covenant promise from Jesus. Use discretion on this section. Call them to believe. If they are not ready, don't push them. If some are ready but not all, set up a time to meet with those who are ready and talk through these questions with them to solidify the gospel and lead them to confession for salvation. In every case, follow-up is necessary to ensure any decision that is made is made for the right reasons and shows a heart of faith to God.
1. Why is your relationship to God broken?
    - I am a sinner: guilty of breaking God's law and deserving of the anger of God to be poured out on me.

2. As the Son-King, who do you believe Jesus is?
    - Jesus is fully God and fully man.

3. As the Servant-King, what do you believe Jesus did to save you?
    - I believe Jesus died in my place to pay my sin debt by cleansing me from my guilt, taking the righteous anger of God against me and covering my shame; credited me with His perfect human righteousness; and rose again to represent me to the Father.

4. Will you call on Jesus for salvation from your sin by repenting of your sin, believing in Jesus's life, death, and resurrection in your place, and submitting to Jesus as your Lord and God?
   *Note: Read Romans 10:9–10, 13 in the learner guide.
   - I repent of my sin, believe in Jesus as my Savior from sin, and submit to Jesus as my Lord and my God.

State to Learners: The Covenant Promise from Jesus
*Note: Read Hebrews 7:25 in the learner guide.
   - If you repent of your sin, believe in Jesus's life and death on your behalf, and submit to Jesus as your risen King and God, your sins will be forgiven, and you will be accepted by God, restored to relationship with God in the kingdom of God.

GLOSSARY

1. Abolish: To put an end to a law or a rule that has been put into place
2. Afflict: To cause terrible mental or bodily pain
3. Altar: A pile of stones on which wood is placed to burn a sacrificed animal
4. Anger of God: God's response to sin that is consistent with the purity of His character and comes out of His righteous rule over His creation
5. Anoint: To set someone apart for a holy purpose (ex. a king)
6. Ascend (v)/Ascension (n):
   - Verb: To go upward
   - Noun: Jesus's exaltation to the Father to sit on the throne and rule over the kingdom of God as the chosen representative of the new humanity.
7. Bear: To take and carry something that is difficult to hold, physically or mentally
8. Believe: To put one's trust in the Lord
9. Burnt offering: An animal sacrifice which symbolized the removal of guilt by the animal dying in the place of the sinner to restore a right relationship with God
10. Call upon the name of the Lord: To come in faith to the Lord for salvation from God's anger through the sacrifice that removes sinners' guilt and covers their shame so that they are restored to relationship with God as their Lord
11. Christ ("anointed one")/Messiah: The promised Offspring of the woman (greater King) who was anointed to defeat sin and death
12. Conceive: The moment a woman becomes pregnant
13. Consecrate: To be set apart as holy for service to God (Mangum, Brown, Klippenstein, and Hurst 2014)
14. Consummate: To have sex for the first time with your spouse after your wedding
15. Corrupt: To damage or destroy something so that it no longer looks like it once did and no longer can do what it was made to do
16. Covenant: An unchangeable agreement that creates a unique relationship between God and man, includes promises and blessings, and requires punishment if the agreement is broken

17. Credit: The act of God adding righteousness to a sinner's relational account with God

18. Criminal: Someone who has broken the law

19. Curse: The act of God speaking judgment on sinners because the covenant has been broken

20. Death: The state of being removed from God's blessing and placed under His curse

21. Descendants: A group of people that comes from a specific person

22. Deserve: To earn something because of one's work

23. Despise: To strongly dislike or hate

24. Disciples: Jesus's closest followers whom He taught and prepared to continue His work

25. Disfigure/mar: To spoil or damage so that someone or something no longer looks beautiful

26. Disgrace: To bring shame on someone

27. Enmity: A feeling of strong hate

28. Establish: To appoint a royal line of kings that will continue forever

29. Exalt: To raise to a higher rank or a more powerful position

30. Expose: To make something known to the public

31. Faith/Faithfully: Trust in the Lord that results in obedience to the word of the Lord

32. Forgiveness: The act of God releasing sinners from a sin debt

33. Forsake: The act of God turning away His love from and pouring out His righteous anger on His Son

34. Fulfill: To complete what was promised in the covenants

35. Gave up His Spirit: To allow (Himself) to die

36. God: The only true God, Creator, and Judge who is separate from everything else and better than everything else

37. Good news/gospel
    - The message of the kingdom of God about the greater Sacrifice of the Messiah

- The truth of who Jesus is and what He did to save sinners through His birth, life, death, resurrection, and ascension

38. Guilt: Responsibility for having done something wrong and especially something against the law (Merriam-Webster 2022)

39. Heal: The act of God restoring the broken relationship (making peace) between God and sinners

40. Heart: The part inside the person that controls how one thinks, desires, and feels

41. Heir: The son who will have legal right to the possessions that belong to a relative when they die; one who will continue the family name

42. High day: The day of a religious festival

43. Holy: Set apart for a special purpose; pure

44. Image: Something or someone that represents the honor, authority, or reputation of someone else

45. Immanuel: God with us

46. Instead of/Substitution: Using something or someone in the place of another thing or person

47. Jealous (God as subject): Extremely protective of someone or something for the good of that person or thing

48. Justice: God's faithfulness to Himself to uphold the law by cursing (requiring full punishment) those who break the law and blessing (giving full reward) those who keep the law

49. Justify: The act of God declaring a sinner righteous/not guilty according to the law of God

50. Lord:
    - The personal name of God that shows Him as having a close relationship with man
    - The personal name of God that shows Him as the covenant-making and covenant-keeping God

51. Lord/Sovereign:
    - The name of God that shows Him as the King with complete authority over all that He created
    - The name of God that shows Him as the King with complete authority who delivers His people from their enemies

52. Lustfully: Having intense sexual want for someone who is not your husband or wife
53. Make intercession: The act of the Servant-King representing sinners to God through His greater sacrifice and His exaltation as the Son-King
54. Mercy: The act of God not punishing a sinner who deserves punishment because He has extended forgiveness
55. Most High: The name of God that shows Him as the highest rank above everything else; the most important
56. Offspring: A person's child
57. Overshadow: The covenantal act of the Holy Spirit covering someone with the presence of God to create new life
58. Paradise: The restored (greater) Garden of Eden where God's people live in God's presence to experience the fullness of His blessing (great beauty, harmony, and peace)
59. Persecute: To cause someone mental or physical hurt because of their beliefs
60. Pierce: To put a hole into something or someone
61. Pledge: To make a promise to a person/group that cannot be broken
62. Pour out: To empty oneself out physically so that a person no longer can continue living
63. Regret (God as subject): To feel great sadness toward someone
64. Reign: The period of time that a king or queen rules over a place
65. Repentance/Repent: The act of turning away from your sin and turning to the Lord as your God and King
66. Represent: To act or speak officially for someone or something
67. Revelation: The act of God making something known that was hidden
68. Righteousness: Right status before the Lord that is based on full obedience to His law and results in right relationship with the Lord (Bankston and Pierson 2019, 59)
69. Rise: To come back to life from death
70. Satisfy: The act of God receiving the full payment that sinners deserve
71. Save/Salvation: The act of God rescuing sinners from His righteous anger
72. Shame: Loss of respect or honor; a feeling of embarrassment because you have done something wrong

73. Sheol/Hell: The place of God's judgment after the death of the physical body where the souls of sinners are separated from His blessing to experience His anger and be punished under His curse with fire
74. Sin: To break God's law
75. Sin debt: Something a person owes God because of their sin
76. Son of man: The ruler who represents mankind to God and establishes the rule of God over the earth (e.g., Adam, Noah, Abraham, and David)
77. Son of Man: The promised Servant-King (Isaiah 53) and Son-King (2 Samuel 7) who represents the covenant people to His Father and establishes the rule of God over the earth
78. Son-King: The greater King, the Son of David and Son of God, who will establish the kingdom of God on earth (Wellum 2021, 60)
79. Symbol: A physical sign (event/word/action) that points to something (idea or spiritual truth) greater or someone greater
80. Ten Commandments: The law of God that describes the unchanging character of God
81. Tomb: A place for people to bury their dead
82. Trustworthy: "Able to be relied on to do or provide what is needed or right" (Merriam-Webster 2022)
83. Virgin: Someone who has never had sex
84. Worship: To give honor to God

BIBLIOGRAPHY

Balz, H. R., and G. Schneider, *Exegetical Dictionary of the New Testament*. Grand Rapids, MI: Eerdmans, 1990.

Bankston, Will and Cheri Pierson. *Exploring Doctrine*. Cumbria, CA3 9WZ, UK: Langham, 2019.

Bible Sense Lexicon. Bellingham, WA: Logos Bible Software, 2014.

Brown, F., S. R. Driver, and C. A. Briggs, *Enhanced Brown-Driver-Briggs Hebrew and English Lexicon*. Oxford: Clarendon Press, 1977.

Carter, Craig. *Interpreting Scripture with the Great Tradition*. Grand Rapids, MI: Baker Academic, 2018.

Harris, R. L., G. L. Archer Jr., and B. K. Waltke (eds.), *Theological Wordbook of the Old Testament*, Chicago: Moody Press, 1999.

Hunter, Trent, and Stephen Wellum. *Christ from Beginning to End*. Grand Rapids, MI: Zondervan, 2018.

Kittel G., G. W. Bromiley, and G. Friedrich (eds.), *Theological Dictionary of the New Testament*. Grand Rapids, MI: Eerdmans, 1964.

Louw, J. P., and E. A. Nida, *Greek-English Lexicon of the New Testament*. New York: United Bible Societies, 1996.

Mangum D., D. R. Brown, R. Klippenstein, and R. Hurst (eds). *Lexham Theological Wordbook*. Lexham Press: Bellingham, WA, 2014.

Merriam-Webster Dictionary. Springfield MA: Merriam-Webster Inc., 2022, https://www.merriam-webster.com/dictionary.

Treat, Jeremy. "The Kingdom of God in 8 Words." *The Gospel Coalition*, May 20, 2019.

Wellum, Stephen J., and Peter J. Gentry. *God's Kingdom through God's Covenant*. Wheaton IL: Crossway, 2015.

Wellum, Stephen J. *The Person of Christ: An Introduction*. Wheaton, IL: Crossway, 2021.

Manufactured by Amazon.ca
Acheson, AB